Disruptive Selling

Disruptive Selling

A new approach to sales, marketing and customer service

Patrick Maes

First published in Belgium in 2016 by Lannoo Publishers as
Disruptive selling: Een nieuwe kijk op sales, marketing en customer service

First published in Great Britain and the United States in 2018 by Kogan Page Limited

2nd Floor, 45 Gee Street	c/o Martin P Hill Consulting	4737/23 Ansari Road
London	122 W 27th St	Daryaganj
EC1V 3RS	New York, NY 10001	New Delhi 110002
United Kingdom	USA	India

© Patrick Maes 2018

The right of Patrick Maes to be identified as the author of this work has been asserted by him in accordance with the Copyright, Designs and Patents Act 1988.

ISBN   978 0 7494 8234 3
E-ISBN   978 0 7494 8235 0

British Library Cataloguing-in-Publication Data

A CIP record for this book is available from the British Library.

Library of Congress Control Number

2017001497

Typeset by Integra Software Services, Pondicherry
Print production managed by Jellyfish
Printed and bound in Great Britain by Ashford Colour Press Ltd.

'I don't want to worry you, but you'll need
a blank sheet of paper.'

CONTENTS

LIST OF FIGURES

LIST OF TABLES

ABOUT THE AUTHOR AND HIS COMPANY

Patrick Maes is CEO of CPI, an advisory bureau for the improvement of commercial performance, with a focus on sales, marketing, customer service and value delivery.

Patrick built up a wealth of experience in the banking world, advertising and industrial consulting before starting his own company, CPI. He is active as lead consultant on a wide range of different projects and regularly gives inspirational talks to companies and organizations on the application of New Sales.

CPI offers an integrated approach for updating your business model and value proposition. This is done through market research and strategy formation. The adjusted business model and value proposition are translated within a single framework into a series of processes, organizational structures, technological innovations and creative concepts.

CPI has four separate activity centres that collaborate to support companies in their transformation to the New Sales model and the new way of working:

- *CPI-Consulting* carries out market research, advises on strategy, business modelling, processes and organization, and draws up quantified change plans.

- *CPI-Technology* provides advice on technological infrastructure with a focus on CRM, marketing automation, business intelligence (BI) and predictive BI.

- *CPI-Lead-builders* develops creative concepts for the positioning and repositioning of companies and products. It plans campaigns for lead generation and customer advocacy, in some cases in collaboration with advertising bureaus or specialist design agencies.

- *CPI-Transformers* helps companies to transform their company culture and to set up a dynamic work environment in which concepts of the new way of working can be applied. It assists with recruiting, onboarding, coaching and the training of managers and staff in sales, marketing and customer service/customer care.

PREFACE

Has it ever crossed your mind that when you place an order with Zalando, book a room with Airbnb or pick up a package from Coolblue that you are functioning as a free worker in a disruptive business model?

These three companies simply serve as examples. There are an increasing number of other companies who are matching supply to demand in a similarly innovative manner. Everyone is interested in the way these companies are changing our industries. They do this by overturning most of the existing conventions relating to the ownership of capital goods, the use of technology and the definition of business activities. However, their disruptive business models also have something else in common: they let their customers do most of the work. Tasks that were previously carried out by an expensive sales apparatus are now pushed on to the consumers.

What's more, these consumers are thrilled and enchanted to get the possibility to be empowered. Their free work results in immediate gratification via 24/7 information, order facilities and tracking services, and these are rated highly by the 21st-century empowered customer.

Disruptive selling calls into question all existing wisdom about commercial organization and the deployment of people and resources in sales, marketing and customer service. Taking it one step further the traditional sales force seems destined for oblivion in the years to come. Sales reps, call centre workers and other intermediaries will become optional, if not wholly unnecessary.

Zalando, Airbnb, Coolblue and other disruptive companies are leading the way in new thinking about sales. Their examples are rapidly gaining ground in traditional companies and in many industries. And this is only the beginning. With the internet of things, products and machines will pass on information about anything relevant to marketeers and service businesses will increasingly base their predictions about future customer behaviour on artificial intelligence. Predictions will be translated into automatically-triggered offers and deliveries.

We are living in an era when we are switching from ownership to use. Customers share their experience of a product or service with other customers, and set up parallel networks of customer care. This creates numerous options for companies that want to drastically reinvent their business model.

In almost all cases these reflections are leading to organizations that are significantly more efficient and customer-oriented than the traditional sales/marketing/service model.

At every level, customer expectations are increasing with regard to the availability of information, access to support services, reaction speed and delivery time, also in B2B. Companies who fail to appreciate this – and fail to act accordingly – can expect to face an increasing lack of understanding from their customers. It is therefore high time to look critically at your own organization and your commercial interaction models.

The good news is that you can achieve much through the use of smart software and affordable technology. People now look at their professional careers in a different way. And social legislation is increasingly focused on the flexible use of human resources. This gives plenty of scope for creativity.

This book will help you with your transformation exercise. It gives you a clear framework and practical guidelines that will allow you to make a start immediately. I will tell you all about the technology and software that can help you. But be warned: you cannot expect to solve all your problems with technology alone.

Successful disruptive selling concepts will be based on the right combination of a series of factors. These include an understanding of what motivates your customers, a corresponding value proposition, appropriate organizational structures and processes and the right culture. This ensures that every contact with your company contributes towards greater *customer advocacy*. The ultimate objective is to make customers happy, by allowing them to work with your company in a rewarding manner. As a result, they will tell other people.

Of course, you must always bear in mind the financial viability of your operations. For this reason, considerable attention will be devoted to matters such as cost to sell and cost to serve. ROMI – return on marketing investment – will never be far from our thoughts.

Technology will continue to evolve. Each year in January, the press and other media channels give an overview of the latest state-of-the-art developments introduced at the Consumer Electronics Show in Las Vegas. This will give you some idea of the speed at which new technologies can be transformed into usable solutions, in almost every conceivable field: from wardrobes that automatically clean and iron your clothes to robots that can replace your company receptionist.

Companies need to accept that change is now a constant in business life. Consequently, it is not enough to question your business model on a single occasion, in the hope that you can continue with it for the next ten to fifteen years. The realities of the market and the demands of your customers will ensure that you need to reassess it continually. The coolest practices in terms of service and customer interaction will be determined by the initiatives of the mainstream disruptors, like Bol.com and Amazon. You will have little option but to adjust and follow – even if you are active in B2B or industrial capital goods.

What you need is a state of mind, an organization and a series of processes that will allow you to respond flexibly to new technological developments and the constantly changing expectations of consumers. Making the right technological choices is crucial. But it is equally important to have the right culture and dynamism within your company.

I would like to share with you how we at CPI assist companies to radically renew their commercial organization and value propositions and help them to remain competitive in both domains. It doesn't matter whether we are talking about financial services, raw materials, machine manufacture, alcohol, cosmetics, chocolate, accounting or insurance. In recent years we have successfully applied the principles contained in this book in each of these sectors.

It is also pleasing to be able to report, not without some pride, that the ideas and practices that we developed here in Antwerp are gradually finding their way into boardrooms throughout Europe. With our disruptive selling approach, we have elaborated a system that can be used universally and on an international scale. The purpose is to create value for companies and their customers. The whole concept of disruptive selling is based on the radical improvement of efficiency, linked to an equally radical improvement in customer-friendliness.

Traditional ways of selling will become the exception. The role of marketing will switch from branding to the generation of qualified leads and the development of brand ambassadors. Customer service will become the hub of relational management. Taking this to its logical conclusion, the traditional profiles of the marketeer, seller and customer service operative will all be called into question. This means that it will become necessary to train these people in a different way.

In this book, I will tell you how you can introduce the concept of disruptive selling into your company. I will show what impact this will have on your customers, your technology and your organizational structures. I will explain how your commercial organization can continue to create value for your customers, before, during and after every interaction. I will demonstrate precisely what marketing automation involves. I will provide a series of handles that will enable you to make the correct choice from the wide selection of marketing toolkits that are available on the market. I will discuss not only the transformation of the sales process, but also the remodelling of your operational structure and your manner of leadership, based on objectives and agreements relating to key results.

In this way, I will draw up a blueprint for a new commercial organization that will offer your customers an authentic, respectful and valuable experience. To make things crystal clear, I will illustrate every aspect of the change process with models and examples.

I hope that the concepts put forward in this book will later find their way into your company, your management team and your staff. I hope, too, that they may also be a source of personal inspiration for your own career development.

For the latest developments, please refer to my blog disruptive-selling.eu, where I post regular updates and presentations relating to sales, marketing and customer service, as well as associated research, metrics and technology matters.

I wish you enjoyable and informative reading!

Patrick Maes

How disruptive is your business already?

On the CPI Consulting website you can test to see how disruptive your sales organization has already become. It only takes a couple of minutes to complete. Afterwards, you receive your score by email.

www.cpi-consulting.eu

Figure 0.1 Take the test

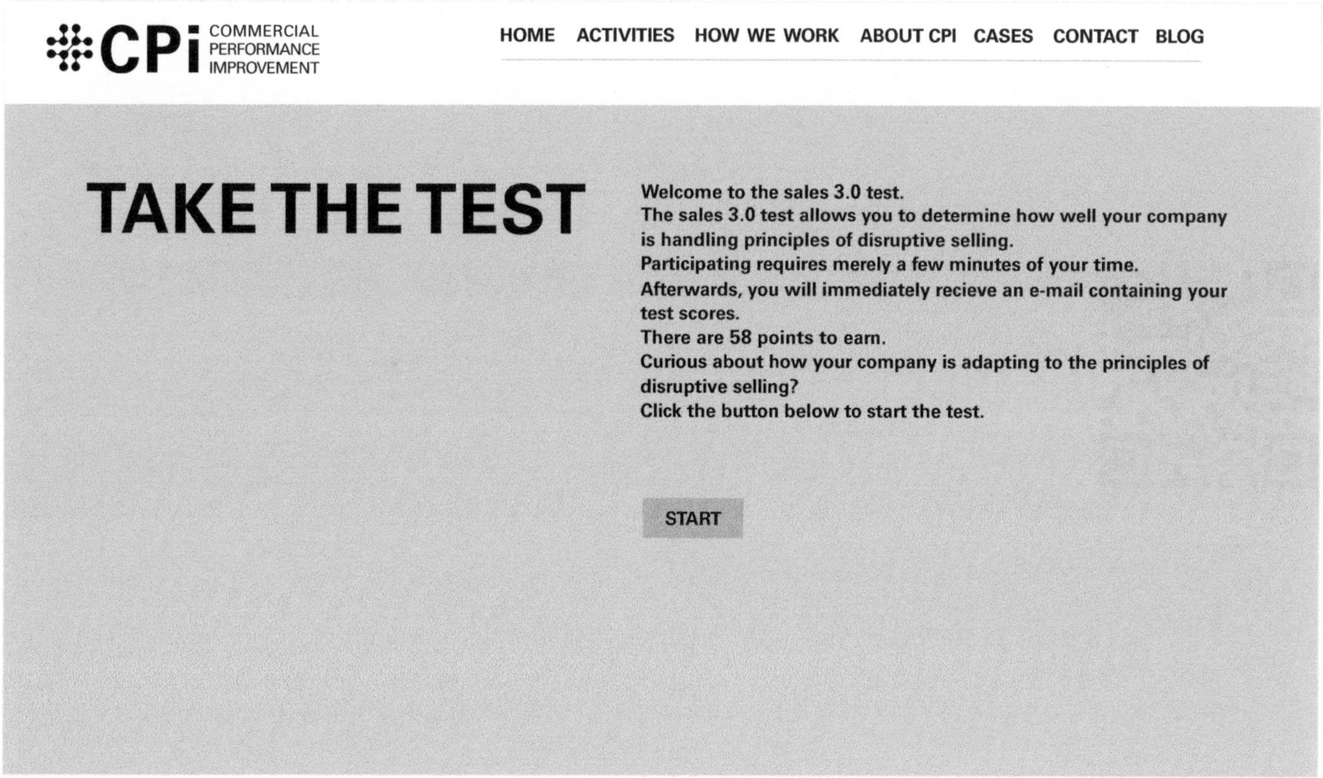
CPi COMMERCIAL PERFORMANCE IMPROVEMENT
HOME ACTIVITIES HOW WE WORK ABOUT CPI CASES CONTACT BLOG
TAKE THE TEST
Welcome to the sales 3.0 test.
The sales 3.0 test allows you to determine how well your company is handling principles of disruptive selling.
Participating requires merely a few minutes of your time.
Afterwards, you will immediately recieve an e-mail containing your test scores.
There are 58 points to earn.
Curious about how your company is adapting to the principles of disruptive selling?
Click the button below to start the test.
START

SOURCE ©CPI-Consulting

Figure 0.2   QR code: Take the test

PART ONE
The end of the world as we know it

Introduction to disruptive selling: start from scratch

Taken from real life

With a blank sheet of paper you begin at zero. And that is what you need to do – start from scratch. Why? Because consumers are constantly changing the boundaries of their expectations. You can see examples of this everywhere. We begin with a story taken from real life, and an example of a company that would also be well advised to conduct a zero-level exercise, to see what it can do better.

The copier

A copy machine. Have you got one in your home? You know the kind of thing I mean. A large, all-in-one, multifunctional copier, which you can use to print, copy, scan, sort, bundle, fold, staple, perforate and fax (another relic of the past!) large volumes of paper. I've got one in my office. It has given me some troublesome moments in its time, but now it has provided me with the inspiration for this chapter.

Let me tell you a story. A few years ago, my then office manager concluded a contract with the supplier of the copier. Every office needs one, and our office was no different. The manager conducted a study beforehand, the main element of which was a comparison of prices: what would it cost and what exactly would this get us in terms of copier, paper, toner, etc.

The firm he finally chose was a specialist firm, active in Benelux and well known for its high-quality technical support. Amongst other things, the contract stipulated how much paper we should use monthly, either for printing or copying. Based on the number of staff in the office and the number of projects in the pipeline, we expected to use about ten thousand sheets of

Figure 0.4   Our copier: a source of inspiration for this chapter

paper each month. This is the figure that was written into the contract. The supplier agreed to send along a maintenance technician at fixed intervals and to provide us with paper and ink cassettes in good time. So far, so good.

In the world of contracts, the purchaser and the supplier are tied to each other. Once the contract has been signed, the conditions governing their relationship become permanent. The wording of the contract determines what goods or services will be provided and at what cost. And in a B2B context, it is not unusual for contracts of this kind to have a duration of five years. But what if circumstances change? What if your company repositions itself after a year of the contract? Or what if you want to introduce a paperless office for environmental reasons? After all, everyone knows that a degree of flexibility is important – and so is the environment!

This is precisely what happened with our company. I decided to push through a major reorganization, so that the paperless office and the New Way of Working could be introduced at CPI. But this meant that instead of 10,000 sheets a month, I now only needed 1,000 sheets maximum. But the copier continued to cost the same 600 euros each month. Yet I had no idea exactly how much I was paying for the different elements of the contract: the leasing of the machine, the use of toner, the use of paper, the maintenance, etc.

If I am not using so much toner, then the supplier doesn't need to deliver it – or so I thought. Similarly, a machine that produces just 12,000 copies a year surely requires less maintenance than a machine churning out 120,000 copies. In the circumstances, it seemed reasonable to ask the supplier to amend my contract. I contacted them and said that I was happy to keep our now excessively large and over-dimensioned copier for the remainder of the leasing period. But I asked that the operating conditions and the monthly cost should be adjusted fairly to reflect the new situation.

Their response to this reasonable request was anything but reasonable. 'Sorry, a contract is a contract. Just see how things develop over the next few months. If you decide at the end of that time that you still don't want the machine, we'll take it off your hands but will regard the remaining monthly payments as compensation for terminating the contract prematurely.'

After several long and not very successful conversations on the phone, I finally received a visit from one of the supplier's sales reps. With a grin on his face, he told me that he had a solution that would save me a lot of money each month. Instead of leasing it for 600 euros a month, from now on we would only be asked to pay just 450 euros a month. This was at least something – but it still left us with a machine that was far too big for our needs and required us to pay over the odds for the minimal use we now had.

As a modern consumer, in the meantime I had done some investigating of my own on the internet. From the various online offers I had received, it was clear that the basic price for just leasing a copier (exclusive of use) was around 150 euros.

Even so, to save further wasted time and effort I decided to cut my losses and accept the offer the rep had made. Imagine my amazement when I read the new contract and discovered that its duration had been increased from 60 to 84 months! At the end of the day, I would end up paying the same total amount of money and would be forced to keep our over-dimensioned monster-copier for a further two years!

To say that I was not happy is an understatement. I was outraged. I vented my frustration on the sales rep, but he said that he had another bright idea that could help to solve our mutual problem: if I would promise to provide him with two or three new customers, he would 'arrange things' with his head office. This 'proposition' – made without the least degree of embarrassment – made me angrier than ever. I told the rep that I never wanted to see him in my company again and that I expected the copier to be removed as soon as possible.

Easier said than done, of course, and for the next few weeks I heard nothing further. Then one day I was called on my voicemail by a friendly sounding lady with a strong Dutch accent. She worked for the supplier company and would like to talk to me. She had been informed about our 'problem' and would like to suggest yet another solution. More in hope than expectation, I picked up the phone and dialled her number. It was an automatic answering system. 'There are currently four calls prior to yours waiting to be dealt with. Please hold the line.' And so I waited. And waited. And waited. After a time, I decided it might be best to try again later.

'There are currently two calls prior to yours waiting to be dealt with. Please hold the line.' Two beats four, and so I did as I was asked. After what seemed like an eternity, I finally got a real live person on the other end of the line. I explained my situation, how I had been called by someone from the company and was now phoning back.' I'm sorry, sir,' I was told politely,' but I don't know what you're talking about. But if it's important, I'm sure they'll call you back. Goodbye – and have a nice day.' And then she was gone!

Finally, the friendly sounding lady – her name was Barbara – did indeed phone me back and we eventually reached a mutually acceptable solution. I agreed to pay 235 euros a month until the end of the lease, and in return they offered a reasonable take-over price for the machine. But while we were negotiating, I still continued to get threatening mails from her colleagues elsewhere in the organization about the invoices on the original contract that I was refusing to pay.

I will spare you the details about the problems we had to actually get the new contract signed. A document with a series of miniscule boxes and equally miniscule text that needed to be filled in by the customer (me) and asked for all kinds of seemingly irrelevant personal information, almost down to my favourite colour and shoe size!

By now, you will probably have guessed that this company is *not* a model of disruptive selling.

It is not simply that they ignore the possible existence of well-informed and empowered customers. They also clearly lack a decent customer relationship management (CRM) system that tells them what has been agreed with customers, when, where and how. As for their sales strategies, these seem to be a throwback to the 1980s – the bad old days, when 'greed was good'.

Since the customer journey in this company (and many others like it) currently has all the comfort of a camel ride and all the predictability of a game of Russian roulette, the management may be well advised to map out and review the different steps of this journey, to see if things can be made simpler, more transparent and more fun. It shouldn't be difficult...

Worst of all, this company is by no means an exception. Countless businesses both great and small still approach sales, customer relations and customer-friendliness from a perspective that is outdated and even counter-productive. Customers are 'hunted'. And once they have been captured, they are held prisoner until they have been bled dry. Every request from the customer to alter this relationship is met with suspicion and/or resistance, almost as a matter of principle. After all, which hunter expects their nicely mounted hunting trophies to start arguing back about the ethics of the hunt or their position on the wall?

The new customer is always right. Even if the contract says they are wrong.

If a company does not find a new arrangement that suits the customer – and find it quickly – the subsequent discussion will be continued on social media. This must be avoided. Every negative post can have a potentially negative effect on possible new customers. In this way, negative posts that drag a company through the mud can ultimately cost much more than simply giving the customer what they want – or at least coming to a reasonable deal.

Returns

During one of our projects with CPI, we compared what it would cost to properly investigate every returned delivery with the cost of simply replacing every returned article without further question. Which of the two options do you think is the cheaper? You've guessed it! Disband your returns police and introduce a 'no questions asked' returns policy. This is not only cheaper, but also has a positive impact on customer satisfaction.

As a result, the company in question not only experienced a rapid growth in sales to existing customers, but also found it easier than in the past to attract new ones.

Which of the two options do you think is the cheapest? You've guessed it!
Disband your returns policy and introduce a 'no questions asked' returns policy.

Customer research indicated that the level of trust given by the company to its customers was an important reason for buying from them, rather than from one of their competitors.

Of course, this does not mean that it is no longer necessary to look at your returns. In this particular case, we decided to process them on the basis of three different categories:

1 'the company's fault';

2 'the customer's fault';

3 'the fault of poor communication'.

There were relatively few instances of 'company error' and 'customer error'. By far the largest proportion of the returns was clearly attributable to defective communication.

This prompted us to link the returns to the customer profiles in the CRM, to see if any particular patterns began to emerge. This revealed that most of the returns came from the company's smaller customers, which did not possess the right software to draw up their orders (for curtain material and curtain hanging systems) online. Instead, they were forced to rely on verbal descriptions and hand-drawn plans of their (often complex) requirements. It was here that things were going wrong. We decided to provide these smaller customers with a new tool. This made it possible to submit clear orders with the right dimensions and all necessary subsidiary information – either by computer or on paper. The number of returned deliveries was drastically reduced.

The company's customer service and marketing departments were mobilized to help persuade the smaller customers to use this new tool. The vast majority of the customers were willing to respond favourably to the proposed change in working practices. This was in large part due to the trust that had already been built up as a result of the 'no questions asked' returns policy.

It goes without saying that this whole operation had a dramatic effect on the efficiency levels of the supplier company. Sales staff were no longer required to visit unhappy customers to explain why their returns were being refused. Customer services wasted less time on trying to decipher near-illegible orders and drawings. The negative energy that had previously been spent on disputing returned goods was transferred into positive energy. This led to a far better working relationship between satisfied staff and satisfied customers.

Disruption – understanding the new way of selling 01

Disruptive selling takes marketing, sales and customer service into a new era. This chapter will explain why. Hopefully, it will help you to get used to the idea. So pull out that blank sheet of paper and let's get started.

Some important questions

Do you sometimes stop to consider the efficiency of your current sales organization? Often, the merest hint of a possible sale is enough to send a rep scuttling out of the office door in the hope of landing a new customer. But the number of visits a rep can make each day is limited.

Research has also demonstrated that customers are showing less and less interest in the classic old-style visit by a company rep[1]. They increasingly regard these visits either as a waste of their valuable time or as an example of the supplier attempting to put them under pressure to buy. Why, they ask, can this kind of thing not nowadays be done online?

Most companies only want to see a rep when it is absolutely essential and in their own interests. Their new motto is: 'don't call us; we'll call you!'

How do you manage your relationship with your customers? Do you know the things that are valuable to each individual customer? Do you know when they are getting ready to make a purchase? Do you know what each customer wants to hear and read? Do you know if they are planning to remain a customer or whether they're contemplating a switch to one of your competitors? Are you monitoring what people say online about your products and your company? And what do you do with all this information?

It is often said that customers are making ever greater demands of their suppliers. This is true. Modern customers decide what is valuable and when it is valuable. If a customer is dissatisfied or feels held to ransom, they are no longer afraid to tell their story to the world. In short, it is demanding customers, with their high level of ever-changing expectation, who now drive and dominate the dynamic of the sales process. Value creation for the customer in today's markets means creating value from the moment a potential lead first indicates interest in a possible purchase. And it continues until long after the sale has been completed.

Making a start

Given this volatile sales environment, it is comforting to know that marketing technology now exists to follow the train of your customers' thoughts seven days a week. As a result, you can gain insights into what they want, what they need and what you can do to provide it.

This book will tell you how to implement this new marketing technology and how to make best use of all its many possibilities. Believe me, you will be amazed. What's more, thanks to this new technology you will have a unique opportunity to increase both your commercial efficiency and your levels of customer satisfaction.

It all starts with the mapping of your customer journey. This means all the various experiences that your customers undergo, from the very first moment they learn about your product, right through to the moment when they are considering a repeat purchase. With this roadmap in your hand, you can identify and eliminate potential bottlenecks, thereby considerably increasing both the ease and the efficiency of the journey. This customer journey is the guiding factor in the remodelling of your sales process. It also shapes the introduction of new sales technology such as marketing automation, social listening and customer relation management (CRM).

Marketing technology allows you to continually optimize the value of your customer experience. Every customer leaves a digital footprint that can tell your sales department a great deal about purchasing needs and intentions. Thanks to marketing automation, it is now relatively easy to monitor this online body language, allowing you to adjust your sales, marketing and after-sales systems in real time. Via the internet of things, smart products and devices will soon be going online, armed with the very latest telematics and an IP address. This will make it possible to track down even more crucial information for the further refinement of your insights into the sales cycle.

New insights

By using all these insights in a fully automated sales approach or by working with a combined approach involving the use of both machines and personnel, you can achieve levels of hyper-personalization and commercial efficiency that were unthinkable in the past.

Once fed with the right information, modern automation tools can segment the market and your customer portfolio in great depth. This makes it possible to approach each customer individually with a made-to-measure care package. Good automation saves both time and money. As a result, it frees up resources that can be used to improve customer service and/or be devoted to increased upselling and cross-selling.

What's more, this is all achieved in a much more targeted, much more efficient and much cheaper manner. Gone are the days when the classic use of CRM to draw up visit reports and a weekly planning schedule was regarded as the ultimate in commercial technology. These new developments give sales staff more room to focus on those moments in the sales process when their knowledge and experience can be used to greatest effect.

In this way, you can build up a marketing system that better understands what your customers want and puts you in a better position to provide it quickly, cheaply and efficiently. This is something that a sales rep, no matter how good, can ever hope to achieve.

The net result is that you will cut costs and increase profits, whilst at the same time making your customers more satisfied than ever before. Lower costs, better results and happier customers: this is the enticing paradox of disruptive selling.

> Lower costs, better results and happier customers: this is the enticing paradox of disruptive selling.

Disruptive selling is taking marketing, sales and customer service into a brand-new era. It is a new sales approach in which the customer takes the lead in a sales process that is largely automated. The introduction of disruptive selling automatically means that the commercial organization of your company will need to be restructured from top to bottom.

The great examples in this new way of doing business, from Amazon to Zalando, all rely heavily on disruptive selling for their success. In these companies, many of the tasks that were traditionally performed by staff in the sales, marketing and customer service departments have now been taken over by mechanized systems.

I am convinced that other companies who remodel their commercial operations by adopting this new approach to sales, marketing and customer service will gain a significant competitive advantage. Companies who react too late will soon find themselves being overtaken by their more prescient rivals. And once they are lagging behind, they will find it very difficult to make up the lost ground[2].

Disruptive selling requires you to start with a blank sheet of paper.

Some SMEs hesitate before introducing radical change in their business methods. They fail to fully appreciate the opportunities that a reorganization of their sales and marketing operations can offer. In part, this is because they overestimate the cost of the transformation; in particular, the technology involved.

A company does not need to be big in order to make its mark in this new sales environment. On the contrary, a starter mentality is a real advantage. The necessary technology, organizational models and business examples are all available to help companies on their way. In particular, the technology has never been cheaper or easier to implement. Remember that Google and Amazon both started as small-scale set-ups. But if you want to follow their example, you will need to reinvent your sales cycle from scratch. Disruptive selling requires you to start with a blank sheet of paper.

To avoid confusion later on, it may be useful at this point to clearly define the following key terms: marketing automation, disruptive selling and CRM.

Marketing automation

Marketing automation is a technology that makes it possible to follow the activities of your customers in real time, 24/7. You can monitor the information they view on your website, the length of time they spend there, what they are buying and not buying, the way they interact with your customer service unit, what they do with mailings and blogs, etc.

Every point of contact that the customer makes with a company provides information that can be analyzed and used. Sometimes the customer provides this information knowingly. Sometimes they do not, unconsciously leaving behind traces of their presence on the internet. In the world of the so-called internet of things, even more additional information will be generated and collated by the sensors contained in smart products that the customer uses.

Marketing automation also makes it possible for all this information to be linked to a series of automatic responses. It sends out triggers that will allow your organization to act quickly when leads are identified and maximize repeat sales from existing customers. In this way, the customer experience is personalized in real time, twenty-four hours a day, seven days a week.

This is a feat beyond the ability of human staff. It is only made possible because the marketing technology is now able to analyse the incoming data automatically and at speed. This data is transformed into in-depth knowledge that can be shared at different levels throughout your organization. This shared knowledge is then used to develop new initiatives, which can either be generated automatically or by the personnel of the sales department.

Disruptive selling

Disruptive selling means that the sales process of a company makes use of every available technological resource to respond as effectively as possible to the needs of the new customer. The technology drives the process. The impact of disruptive selling will require fundamental change in your sales approach. This will involve the disappearance of the current boundaries between sales, marketing and customer service, so that the sales process can be managed as an integrated whole. This means interacting continuously with customers from the moment they first learn about your product to the moment they are considering a repeat purchase.

The objective is to so pamper customers that they motivate themselves to make purchases, effectively becoming their own salesperson, with you as sales manager.

There are many different definitions of the term 'disruptive'. We take it to mean the radical redefinition of the crucial link between customers and value propositions without the hindrance of existing structures and conventions and with the maximum use of all available technological tools, supported by the smart deployment of people and other resources. Disruptiveness makes it possible to do things that people alone cannot do.

Just as the disruptive business model of Uber makes no use of its own taxis, it is perfectly possibly that in future you will generate a bigger turnover with fewer staff – or perhaps even with no staff at all. What's more, because the relevant technologies are usually found in the cloud, you don't need to own or develop them. This will revolutionize the traditional sales models of the past, allowing a more flexible and targeted response to the changing patterns of customer expectation.

A sales process making use of marketing automation – especially in combination with big data and the internet of things – will inevitably be disruptive.

> Disruptive selling is a self-reinforcing process. By collating and analysing more information to provide targeted information to your customers and your own commercial organization, your company will systematically get better at what it does.

Disruptive selling makes it possible to do the same amount of work with fewer people. It also allows you to use your scarce and expensive of human resources where they are most needed. As a result, a higher turnover is generated, but the automation of the acquisition and value delivery processes means that costs will be significantly reduced.

Disruptive selling is a self-reinforcing process. By collating and analysing more information to provide targeted information to your customers and your own commercial organization, your company will systematically get better at what it does.

CRM

Customer relationship management (CRM), as the name implies, is a tool that allows you to manage and follow up your relations with your customers. CRM makes it possible to neatly catalogue all your individual customers into typologies or segments, so that you can plan, implement and monitor your various interactions with them.

CRM started life as a relational database, but has been systematically developed to become a fundamental enabler in the sales process. CRM asks questions. It makes suggestions about possible sales initiatives. It ensures that all levels of the organization approach the customer or prospect as part of a single entity (the company), rather than as a series of individual units (sales, marketing, etc).

Unfortunately, CRM has a bad reputation with some companies. This is because the old CRM packages were based on the wrong angle of approach. They were developed first and foremost as IT projects, with little real understanding of the sales process and with the fairly limited objective of providing the sales teams with a list of things to do each day. The interfaces were user-unfriendly and it was often only possible to consult information by calling in to servers that that were not always readily accessible.

In contrast, today's CRM systems are quick, easy and even fun to use, and can be linked to all standard electronic devices. The implementation of these new systems is based on a thorough knowledge of current sales and marketing processes. When you choose a system, the added value of the insights it offers your users in terms of these processes should be the key criterion – not the level of control it gives or the number of reports it produces.

Nowadays, CRM is largely cloud-based and there are numerous options with a wide range of different possibilities, interfaces and prices.

Other tools

Figure 1.1   Social listening

SOURCE ©CPI-Consulting

Before you embark on your disruptive selling project, it will be useful to also have a number of other tools at your disposal. These not only include the so-called social listening tools – systems that permit you to follow everything said about your company on social media in real time – but also internal communication tools such as Yammer, Slack and Yamla.

You will also need organizational and management concept tools such as Objectives and Key Results (OKR). These tools will allow the new concepts to be introduced into your company smoothly and efficiently. You can either buy these tools for yourself or have them installed by specialist companies like CPI.

Many of the examples in this book are drawn from websites. However, in this context the concept of a website should be interpreted in a broad sense. Various apps and other digital outlets are also involved. The general 'appification' of the customer journey is gaining ground quickly and will soon be the default set-up for most companies. This opens up scope for the development of a whole new branch of marketing automation for tracking the use of different apps.

Nowadays, even the Vatican has its own app – Patrum – which allows you to conduct a virtual tour of the Vatican Museum. In our app-mad world, it will not be long before companies will be forced to consider the use of mobile marketing as an integral part of their overall commercial approach.

Notes

1   Maes, Patrick (2014) *Turn Opportunity into Sales Results*, CPI-Consulting
2   Maes, 2014

Creating connections with the new customer through disruptive selling

02

The new customer is critical, and expects more and different, as do professionals in the B2B market. The customer takes the lead in the sales process.

Copycat behaviour

Read any blog or recent book about consumer behaviour, and they will all confirm that today's customers are better informed than ever before. This is hardly surprising: the modern mobile customer has 24/7 access to a vast store of information – and makes use of it.

The relevant figures in the research vary on this matter, depending on the product on the customer's wishlist. Even so, we can still conclude that at least 75 per cent of prospects first view all the information about their chosen product online before they even think about contacting a sales outlet. In fact, today's customer is often better informed than the sales staff!

In these circumstances, the message is clear: as a supplier, you can no longer compel the customer to keep on picking your company. The customer will make their own choice. Long live the free customer! Various studies have shown that customers complete between 30 and 70 per cent of their customer journey before they actually get around to making real choices. Suppliers who fail to make this journey with the customer will have little chance of winning a new order.[1]

> 75 per cent of prospects first view all the information about their chosen product online before they even think about contacting a sales outlet.

The modern customer is searching for new value and for a new purchasing experience. It is no longer enough simply to provide a perfect product or service. Your competitors are doing that as well. Similarly, the new forms of technology are readily available to all, so tech alone cannot make the difference.

As a result, the sales story is no longer exclusively about what you offer the customer in material terms. The 'softer' elements of your value proposition, including customer service, are often the only way to distinguish yourself from your rivals. Customers are more and more inclined to choose products and services on the basis of this extra value. Before too long, customer service in B2B will be more important than price or product in your battle to differentiate your company from its competitors.[2]

The customer wants to be part of the process so that they can compile their own 'made-to-measure' package of material and immaterial benefits – not only at the moment of sale, but from the very first moment they start to gather information about the product or service, and throughout the entire purchase and usage period. The customer has taken the lead in the sales process – and has no intention of surrendering it.

The contemporary customer journey therefore involves much more than a straightforward purchase of a product or service. It is also about the way the service is provided or the product is maintained; about the way problems and discussions are dealt with; about the way the customer connects with the supplier company and its other customers. In short, it is about genuine customer-orientation.

This new sales process also requires a new way of selling. In fact, selling is a thing of the past. We are now in the age of 'selping', a combination of selling and helping[3] – or as we describe it at CPI: 'Inspiring, Enchanting and Sustaining'.

> The minimum expectations of the customer are determined by the companies and brands which set the coolness norm.

What the customer regards as reasonable – in other words, their minimum expectations – are nowadays determined by the companies and brands which set the coolness norm. If customers are given the opportunity to configure products online, given a warm 'thank you' for placing an order, kept fully informed at every stage about the progress of that order, informed precisely about where and when the delivery will be made, and invited immediately after that delivery to give an opinion about the product and the company's service, then very quickly all these things will soon come to be regarded as standard.

In this way, the customer learns that speed is not impossible; that 'easy' is not a difficult word; that correct treatment is the most normal thing in the world; that their ideas count and their comments are appreciated. The removal of every obstacle is the secret to the best possible earning model for the supplier company.

When you place an order with Zalando, you can simply send back anything you don't like. When you order a taxi via Uber, you can access an app that shows you the opinions of past customers about the rides on offer at any given moment – and afterwards you can add your own opinion to the list.

Even the word 'purchase' is sounding ever more hollow. A purchase is so final. Streaming, subscribing or becoming a member of a community is much more flexible. Why fill up your cupboard with DVDs if you can watch the entire series via Netflix? If you order a new book from Amazon and it arrives with a crease, all you need to do is send them a simple mail. When this happened to me, I received an answer within an hour and within days they had sent me a new book, no questions asked. I was allowed to keep the creased version and they even suggested I might like to pass it on to somebody else!

Of course, the people at Amazon know that there is a good chance that I will also pass on the story about my 'free' book – and that is what they are counting on.

Time to scream

In 2011, Zalando made a series of fun films about the reactions of customers when their Zalando package is delivered to their doorstep – the so-called *Time to Scream* commercials.

Ever since, we at CPI refer to a 'Zalando experience' whenever we think of something that we believe will so delight the customer that he/she will want to share the moment via social media. In other words, the Zalando effect is a yardstick for assessing expected levels of customer enchantment.

Owners of clothes stores and bookshops who want to react to the growing online threat to their business need to do more than simply open their own online shop. To begin with, they need to find a way to translate the entire experience provided by their online competitors into the physical environment of their shop.

But they also need to add a little something extra that will allow them to outshine their digital rivals: 'If you're not happy with that dress, just bring it back! You've already worn it and thrown away the ticket? No problem: we know exactly what all our customers have bought. Perhaps you'd like a cup

Figure 2.1 Infographic: The impact of social media

It is not only young people who are involved.

49,5% 44,6% 37,5% 31,7% 27,4%

18-24   25-34   35-44   45-54   55+

Percentage of people from the different age groups who have had contact with a brand via social media.

68% of people who use social media say that it has helped to determine their opinion about the brand.

65% think that social media are more useful than call centres when it comes to asking questions.

This is nine times more than the number of peopl who felt less well informed after using social media.

Only **7%** think that call centres are better than social media.

40% Think that social media improve customer service.

This is six times more than the number who think that the use of social media leads to worse customer service.

SOURCE ©CPI-Consulting, based on data from Warc[5]

Figure 2.2   Infographic: The new customer

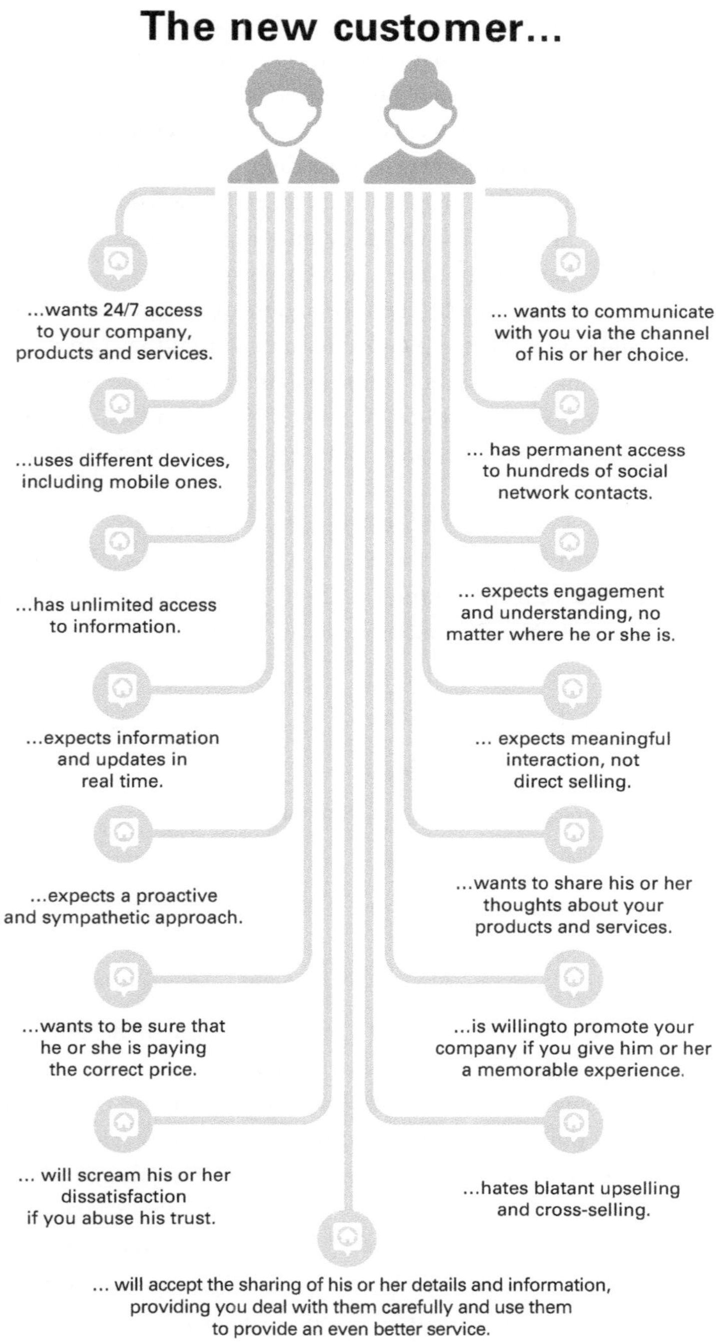

The new customer...

...wants 24/7 access to your company, products and services.

... wants to communicate with you via the channel of his or her choice.

...uses different devices, including mobile ones.

... has permanent access to hundreds of social network contacts.

...has unlimited access to information.

... expects engagement and understanding, no matter where he or she is.

...expects information and updates in real time.

... expects meaningful interaction, not direct selling.

...expects a proactive and sympathetic approach.

...wants to share his or her thoughts about your products and services.

...wants to be sure that he or she is paying the correct price.

...is willingto promote your company if you give him or her a memorable experience.

... will scream his or her dissatisfaction if you abuse his trust.

...hates blatant upselling and cross-selling.

... will accept the sharing of his or her details and information, providing you deal with them carefully and use them to provide an even better service.

SOURCE ©CPI-Consulting

of coffee while you are browsing? Or maybe some colour advice?' 'Great idea – if only I had the time! Perhaps I'll have a look at home via your app. You do have an app, don't you?'

A good illustration of the way customer expectation is increasing is the growing anger over classic customer loyalty cards. Even if the card is fitted with a chip, customers are still dissatisfied. As a result, the responsibility for keeping customer details and for paying out the discount in a proactive and transparent way has been shifted from the customer to the company. This means that the cards – no matter how fancy and sophisticated – and the procedures attached to them are becoming increasingly obsolete.

The modern customer also wants to be involved in creating value. *LEGO design by me* lets children play with LEGO software, so that they can design their own LEGO building kits. And if you think this co-creative process is confined to just the kids, you would be wrong! LEGO also has an online 'mindstorms community', where members can help to write the software for LEGO robotics.

giffgaff is another good example. This British telecom operator is a spin-off of O2, which in turn is part of the Spanish Telefónica conglomerate. The brand was launched onto the market in 2010 as a kind of experiment. Today, it has a remarkable Net Promoter Score of 73 per cent[5].

Figure 2.3   Infographic: Net Promoter Score

Net promoter score = % promoter – % detractors

SOURCE ©CPI-Consulting

Right from the very start, it was giffgaff's bold ambition to be both the cheapest and to provide the best customer service on the market. Most companies – and customers – would probably think that these two objectives are incompatible. But not giffgaff – and they managed to achieve their dual goal by making their giffgaff community central to everything they do.

There are no customers, only community members, who help each other in whatever way they can and also encourage their family and friends to become new members. There is no call centre. Only questions relating to payment are dealt with directly by giffgaff, and always by mail. All technical questions are answered by other community members, via telephone or chat, peer-to-peer. And this usually happens within 90 seconds[6].

Those who help others in this way are rewarded, firstly via a system of discounts on their own telephone bill. Once this initial amount has been used, additional credits can be donated to a charity of the customer's choice. Later, it is possible for members to earn extra income up to a certain maximum.

giffgaff also offers online training to teach its members how they can best help others.[7] Members who think they have reached expert level can test themselves by taking part in a quiz. This makes it possible to distinguish experienced helpers from hardcore helpers.

In short, an entire community has been built up around the brand. This offers a platform where new ideas are posted for extending the service and where much more is discussed than simply the merits of the latest smartphone. It is even possible to vote for particular ideas, which gives them added value and worth. To date, no fewer than 14,000 ideas have been posted, some 10 per cent of which have been implemented by giffgaff.

The O2 telecom company has also attracted customer and media interest in other ways. One of its most innovative ventures was the well known 'Be more dog' campaigns. This was a series of hilarious commercials in which it was claimed that dogs have more fun in life than cats because they always yield to their impulses, whereas cats are more careful and calculating.

This basic idea was translated into a formula that allows customers to acquire the latest smartphone at minimal cost – and without any inhibitions – simply by exchanging their current phone. Of course, this brilliant promotional stunt was supported by an equally brilliant publicity campaign on social media, which allowed you to calculate your own 'be more dog' score and share it with others.

When the pundits write about changing customer expectations, the subject is most commonly viewed from the perspective of the consumer. They usually refer to the Amazons, Zalandos, Ubers, LEGOs and Netflixes of the world. These are all companies who started from nothing and have turned classic business models upside down by shaping new consumer expectations in a disruptive manner. They also mention the consequences of this revolution for traditional selling methods and distribution channels.

And to be honest, I also use these same examples – but with an important qualification: what consumers are currently experiencing in their own lives as private individuals, they will soon come to expect in their professional lives as well. If you fail to offer disruptive experiences in B2B, somebody else will do it in your place. In fact, customers might even do it themselves.

If you fail to offer disruptive experiences in B2B, somebody else will do it in your place.

Figure 2.4 O2's Be More Dog campaign

SOURCE O2, with kind permission of VCCP

Cheap train travel in the Netherlands with grouptickets.nl

Letting the customer know that you are interested in them: that's the name of the game. Student Alexandru Bondor from the Dutch city of Zwolle was fed up paying for expensive train tickets every time he wanted to visit his girlfriend in Utrecht. But he soon found a solution – in the small print of the group travel arrangement offered by the Dutch National Railway Service (NS).

Two years ago, the NS introduced a group ticket that allowed groups of friends, societies, sports clubs, schools, etc to make cheaper journeys to the same destination. However, the regulations did not state that all the members of the group need to get on at the same station, or even that they need to take the same train. Using this loophole, computer programmer Bondor developed the app groupstickets.nl.

The app is as simple as it is ingenious. All you need to do is log in to a Facebook account, choose a destination, and join the group that is travelling to that same destination on the same day. If there is currently no group for the destination in question, the user can make a new group themselves and post it online.

As soon as a group of ten people has been formed, one of them purchases the tickets from ns.nl. The buyer then sends the tickets to the other members of the group, as soon as they receive a screenshot to prove that they have been reimbursed the price of the ticket. Using this clever system, a return ticket from Zwolle to Utrecht costs just 7 euros instead of the usual 29. 80 euros![8]

The site has been online since May 2015, and in less than six months had no fewer than 64,000 registered users.

And how did the NS respond to this inventive initiative? They confirmed that they were aware of the existence of grouptickets.nl. They also pointed out that it was not initially their intention to encourage the creation of special groups to take advantage of the lower fares. Martijn Kamans, a spokesman for the NS, said: 'The group return was intended to attract new customers who would not otherwise use the train outside of peak hours. However, it now seems that it is groups of existing customers who are profiting from the system.'

'Having said that, we welcome every form of publicity for our group returns. We have made contact with Mr Bondor and will be discussing with him how we can best serve and strengthen each other's interests.'[9]

In the meantime, a deal has been brokered and Bondor has agreed to terminate his initiative. Even so, it remains an excellent example of the way consumers can cause surprises for companies through the power of social media.

Railway companies often have problems with creative solutions that they did not think of themselves, but are popular with the public. When a number of Belgian commuters with computing expertise devised an app to check train timetables, it quickly became more widely used by travellers than the state railway company's own app. As a result, the company took out an injunction to have the private app removed from the internet, arguing successfully that train times are part of their intellectual property. A small victory in principle for the company, but a huge moral loss of face in terms of its public reputation.

The unconscious barriers to customer satisfaction

Companies put a surprising number of barriers in the way of their business customers. This often happens unconsciously – not that this is any consolation to the unhappy and confused customer. These barriers are usually a result of an exaggeratedly process-based approach to administrative matters. Every company likes to control its own business – at least to a degree. To achieve this, it devises a series of procedures, decision-making criteria and levels of authority.

At a physical level, this is translated into the creation of different departments and services, each with their own rules, regulations and guidelines: barriers which their staff are taught to monitor and uphold. Not surprisingly, this results in an approach in which the company itself is central – which can be a major problem when you need to switch to an approach where the customer is central.

Many of these barriers are maintained simply as a reflex to protect income and jobs. Question: why do you need that particular stamp? Answer: because it is somebody's job to use it, a task for which the company can justifiably charge. Question: why can't that estimate be calculated digitally at no cost? Answer: because then the company wouldn't need its impressive array of spreadsheets and flowcharts, which again requires someone to make them and again can be legitimately charged to the customer.

Companies don't like to keep things small and simple. They need to show that customers are getting plenty of effort for their money: and all too often this means large and complex.

Once empowered, always empowered

There was once a time when an accountant managed your accounts and sent you a monthly invoice for their services. What the accountant actually did for this money always remained a secret. Once a year, they would organize a brief consultation meeting, when they would tell you how much profit (or loss) you had made and how much you would have to pay the taxman. Of course, they would then also send you an extra invoice for this privilege of receiving this information.

This type of approach is becoming increasingly unacceptable to customers. An accountant is a supplier like any other, and there are dozens to choose from. The accountant who wants to make a difference will therefore need to appeal to the newly empowered customer by asking: 'Dear customer, what can I really do to help you?' or 'Dear customer, how do you see our relationship in the future?'

Customers – even an accountant's customers – now expect to be able to choose from a range of services: 'yes' to this, this and this, but 'no' to that, that and that. And if they want to change their mind on a regular basis, this needs to be possible as well. The organization, processes and marketing of modern-day accountancy need to reflect these new realities.

If you want a new accountant, you will probably start by searching on the internet. Once you have a selection of possible candidates, you will most likely check with your network to see what your contacts have to say about your initial choices. Using their comments and suggestions, you will then draw up a list of criteria that you will use to assess the remaining candidates. These might include flexibility (the free choice of accounting software, etc); what standard packages are on offer; optional extra services that are available (asset management, fiscal control, etc) – and last but not least, the cost.

Once you have established these criteria, you can easily test them company by company online.

Nowadays, it only takes a couple of hours for a consumer to conduct a do-it-yourself market study of this kind. With just a few clicks of your mouse you can find out all sorts of useful information. The reverse side of this coin is that an accountant without a clear and attractive website is no longer an accountant of any standing. People now expect accountants to be 100 per cent transparent. In today's world, this means posting online all the information – including a price list – that will allow comparison with other accounting colleagues.

This has reduced accountants to the same status as every other supplier. In other words, they need to think about customer expectation at every moment of the customer journey. Only in this way will they be able to decide where their office is able to make a real difference. The accountancy firms that wish to grow in the future will be those who appeal to the wishes of the empowered customer by offering them real added value in key areas of specific concern.

Cross-contamination

It is only reasonable to suppose that the expectations which are now standard in the consumer market will soon become the norm in B2B and industrial marketing as well. For example, the journey that a professional customer takes with their accountant – a supplier like any other – is probably not so different from the journey taken when booking the tickets for a holiday online with a low-cost airline like Ryanair.

At Ryanair, the entire range of services is split up into individual service elements, for each of which the customer pays separately. In this sense, the company accepts that the customer will have absolute flexibility to lead the sales process. The standard ticket is with hand luggage alone. If you want to take more luggage, you can – but you pay more. The same is true of insurance, preferential seating, car hire, etc.

The Ryanair website makes all these matters crystal clear to its customers – and it is always the customer who indicates what they do and do not want. It is quick, easy and flexible. At the same time, it allows Ryanair to put a large part of the administrative burden (and its cost) onto the shoulders of the customers. Not that this burden is a particularly severe one. With the advent of digital check-in cards, it is not even necessary to print out your ticket.

Of course, this same principle can also be applied to many other circumstances where documents are necessary. And once travellers get used to paperless journeys, they will increasingly want to see the same thing in a work context. For many people, a digital version of the necessary document on their smartphone will suffice. And if someone in your company answers 'sorry, we don't do that here', you are soon going to find yourself in difficulties.

For customers who forget to put a tick in the right box, it is important to always offer an acceptable solution – for a price, of course. In this way, these extra transactions are not an encumbrance for companies like Ryanair, but are actually a source of additional revenue.

Modern business models take no account of the artificial division between B2C and B2B.

Ryanair also has many professional customers, companies who are anxious to cut their travelling costs and therefore now order their tickets via the company computer. The same is true for Airbnb. Why should you make a B2B booking with a hotel for your business trip when you can make a cheaper C2B booking with a private individual? This also applies to professional literature, which is nearly always bought via Amazon or Bol.com rather than from the more expensive publishing houses.

Modern business models take no account of the artificial division between B2C and B2B, between ordinary consumers and professional customers. In this way, they contaminate the cultural expectations of the professionals whenever they go in search of their requirements.

B2B and B2C are coming together

The differences between the sales process in B2C and B2B are becoming increasingly vague – and the speed of this change is remarkable. As customers, our mobile technology means that we now have access to a limitless mine of information twenty-four hours a day, seven days a week. What are you looking for? A new microwave, a new car, a new machine or a new supply of raw materials? In most cases you will begin your search for possible suppliers on Google, on your computer, tablet or smartphone.

In this respect, the attitude and approach of the customer when buying a machine, engaging a service or choosing an accountant is broadly the same as when they buy a book or reserve a hotel room online. In all these cases, expectations are comparable, if not identical.

Some people might say that the customer in a B2C sales process has increasingly less contact with the supplier or commercial organization, particularly in an online context. In contrast, this contact is nearly always present in the B2B sales process. But is this really the case? And even if it is, will it stay that way?

The number of B2B transactions conducted online is also increasing rapidly. The intervention of human staff is now often restricted to problem situations that the automated systems cannot solve. The distinction between B2C and B2B can perhaps still be defended on the basis of the different methods of financial settlement: one using a simple cash receipt, the other a formal invoice. That being said, nowadays we nearly all make our payments electronically or online. And whether you make the payment from the couch in your living room or from your office chair at work makes very little difference in the end.

Perhaps the B2B purchase process is a little more structured and involves more people than B2C, since within companies the various responsibilities are divided and process-based. But you could say much the same for an important domestic purchase, where several members of the family may be involved in making and implementing the purchase decision.

> What the consumer experiences in their private life, they will (soon) want to experience in their professional life as well.

The empowerment of the customer first started in the consumer market. In this market, every barrier to customer comfort and customer satisfaction has been gradually removed, so that the customer is now in charge of the sales process. And now that this pleasing idea has been planted in our minds, we naturally want more.

As a result, we no longer make an artificial distinction between what we want as a consumer and what we want as a business professional. If you need a new machine or a new type of raw material, why shouldn't you have the opportunity to test the various options first, keeping the most suitable and returning the rest? It is simply a natural evolution: what the consumer experiences in their private life, they will (soon) want to experience in their professional life as well. Once people are contaminated by an idea, they stay that way!

I have deliberately put the word 'soon' in brackets. I don't want to rush you into things. I would prefer you to get used to the idea at your own speed. But I would certainly suggest that you should already investigate your own personal pattern of expectations, because there is a good chance that what you expect as a consumer you will eventually come to expect in a business environment. You might not get it yet – but you almost certainly want it!

CASE STUDY

Buying a €77,100 car is now something you do online

A good example of disruptive selling is the way that Tesla interests its potential customers in its Model 70D. At the bottom of the company's promotional emails it has buttons saying 'Test drive' and 'Order now'. Buying a car that costs €77,100 with just the click of a mouse? Yet it works!

If you click on the 'order' button, you enter a very clear environment. Everything you need to do is explained simply, step by step, up to and including the payment of a first instalment. To give any waverers the last little push they need, the site also explains about the company's buy-back policy at a guaranteed price and various options such as 'Tesla arranged financing', 'financing through my bank' and 'pay later or by Wire Transfer'.

What implications does this kind of online sale have for the brand concession holders, with their large and expensive car showrooms? Will people still want to come to the showrooms? What will happen if they don't? Overall vehicle sales may remain the same, but what about the showroom staff, who will probably have much more time on their hands than before? Can they be found other things to do, or will they be shown the door?

According to Educam, the knowledge and training centre for the automobile sector in Belgium, in 2008 the average customer visited a showroom 4.3 times before they made a purchase. By 2012, that had fallen to just 1.3 times.[10] Educam's Route 2020 study sketches their forecast for the future of the Belgian car industry. They conclude that it will become increasingly difficult to earn money from the sale of cars. As a result, they predict that if the sector does not change its earning model, by 2020 some 20 per cent of the current jobs in the industry will be lost.

'Nowadays, just 5 per cent of customers are brand loyal. They enter a showroom with a fixed idea in their mind: "This is the car I drive now, I am happy with it, and so I will stay with the same make." The other 95 per cent all go online to scan the market for what's new or better,' says Luc De Moor, managing director of Educam.[11]

'Of the 95 per cent who go online, 30 per cent do it on a mobile device, not on a computer. This means that car websites need to be compatible for use with mobile devices. If I want to check something about your car but can't find it on my smartphone, there's a good chance I will cross you off my list.

'So what's the best way to influence the seekers? You need to invest heavily in data management and learn as much as you can about your potential customers and their behaviour. In contrast to the past, car sellers now need to create a double bond: car plus customer.'

According to De Moor, the future earning model for the sector needs to focus on perfect after-sales follow up. 'Nowadays, cars are smartphones on four wheels. In my dealership, I have a control room where I can follow the data being transmitted from every car I have sold. If the control room operator sees that a band sensor has been activated, we can contact the owner with a tailor-made proposal for new tyres. Or perhaps suggest that now is a good moment to switch to winter tyres.'

De Moor is right in his analysis. His only mistake is to think that you still need an operator. You don't. Sending messages to the customer in response to warning signals can be fully automated. So too can the making of maintenance appointments, the arrangements for replacement cars, etc.

Much the same is true of the follow-up for customer searches online. Analysing what interests them, following up leads, sending out targeted invitations at just the right moment and so on can all be done automatically. So where do the sales staff fit in to all this? With the time they save and with the help of all these extra analyses, their task in the future will be to deepen the interaction between the potential customer and the brand/showroom. They will do this by approaching each customer in a highly personalized way.

Learning to look at things in a new light

As a commercial B2B, it is not difficult to find a new pair of spectacles that will allow see things differently. In fact, you don't even need a pair of spectacles. There are already dozens of examples just waiting to be followed. Just make sure you don't stick your head in the sand – be open to new ideas and learn to look at things in a new light. That's all it takes to turn opportunities into sales results!

The first golden rule is that your product must always do what it promises. It must be specific, conforming and traceable, as well as complying with all other requirements, legal and otherwise. However, this is probably also true of your competitors' products.

In some cases, it may be possible to make a difference through creative technical innovation. But it is more likely that in future the best way to differentiate your company from the rest will be through the excellence of the experience you are able to offer your customers. In short, you need to make it easy and fun to buy your product. 'Easy' and 'fun' are two important reasons why customers keep coming back for more.

Today's customers are constantly searching for new value. So why not give it to them in a form that saves time and keeps them entertained?

'Easy' and 'fun' are two important reasons why customers keep coming back for more.

For example, why are there so few practical tips or informative messages on cardboard boxes and other packaging? Tips such as: 'If you follow the folding lines, you can turn me into a handy tray' or 'Thanks for using our product! If you have any comments or ideas that can help us to serve you better, please let us know by scanning the QR code'. And speaking of QR codes, why do you so seldom find one on the packaging of machines, etc? This could easily be linked to a how-to-use video, which would save the customer both time and effort.

Far-fetched? Not really. In supermarkets, the use of QR codes and near-field communication (the information made available on your smartphone via Bluetooth) is rapidly becoming commonplace.

Scan your crab

QR codes are used by king crab supplier Norway King Crab in a creative and original way. Scan the code attached to your king crab and you immediately get an abundance of useful information, including the weight of the crab, the name and a photo of the fisherman, and even a film of the stretch of water between Antarctica and Finland where the crab was caught!

Figure 2.5 A practical application of near-field communication by Norway King Crab

SOURCE Norway King Crab (Photo: Natasha Fedorova)

The customer's experience will decide whether they want to help make or break your brand.

The behaviour of a professional customer no longer differs significantly from the behaviour of an ordinary consumer. The days are long gone when the customer – whether private or professional – was only concerned about the nature and performance of the product or service. Nowadays, they are equally interested in the atmosphere surrounding the entire purchase experience.

This interest runs from the moment when they first come into contact with the product or service, right up to the moment when they decide to replace it. The modern customer wants to choose for themselves. And they don't want to be limited in that choice – they want to take well-informed decisions and to keep their options open as long as possible.

In today's market, it is the customer who sets the minimum demands. The supplier must meet these demands, if it wants to remain in the running with competitors for a possible sale. What's more, the demands are getting bigger all the time. The customer not only wants reliable quality, prompt delivery and excellent customer support, but also expects to be constantly surprised, entertained and enchanted. There is no excuse for being boring – and God help you if you are!

There is no excuse for being boring

Many companies are still not aware of this. They fail to understand that customers now take a 360° view, drawing in information from every possible source. The number of suppliers who bury crucial documents and information so deep in their website that only the most persistent prospect will ever find them is still surprisingly large. Many of these websites also have a disturbing lack of transparency. Often, they still fail to include a price list or a comments and complaints file.

Companies continue to think far too much in terms of sales. As a result, they overlook the new key components in the modern recipe for market success: identifying and living up to the customer's expectations. Suppliers need to understand what their customers are feeling. They must provide the added value that the customer needs (and is willing to pay for) at that particular moment in their relationship.

A company that is able to lead the way in translating customer expectations into outstanding service provision will also create the same expectations for its competitors. This will allow that company to distinguish itself from the rest, at least initially. In particular, it says much about the company's positive culture and its genuine desire to create happy customers.

This is closely related to concepts such as Triple-A – authentic, accountable and agile – and Customer Service Wildcards, which we will be examining more closely later in the book.

CASE STUDY

The FREITAG experience

If you order a bag from FREITAG, they continue to send you fun mails and wacky photos long after your purchase has been completed.

FREITAG, a company founded by the Swiss brothers Markus and Daniel Freitag, has been making designer bags and rucksacks since 1993. Its unique concept makes use of old lorry tarpaulins, recycled safety belts and bicycle inner tubes. Each year, FREITAG reprocesses some 390 tons of redundant tarps, 15,000 bicycle inner tubes and 150,000 belts.

Figure 2.6   FREITAG also offers customer service for injured or geriatric bags

SOURCE ©Noë Flum, used with kind permission from FRETAIG

In reality, FREITAG can only provide this personalized and perfectly timed customer experience thanks to its far-reaching market automation. These systems make use of information contained in the order form to send fun messages that will make the delivery time pass more quickly and more amusingly. At the same time, this helps to further strengthen their brand reputation.

Compare the FREITAG experiences with the following scenario, which is typical to all too many online stores. To start with, you are asked to choose between model A, model B, model C or model D. You are then asked to click on a preferred colour – for example, blue, silver or yellow – before registering your delivery details and moving on to the payment formalities. This usually requires the filling in of a number of codes, none of which you ever have to hand. And once you have finally completed everything, all you get in return is a brief message saying 'We have received your order. Thank you'.

If you want to follow the progress of the order, you need to log in again to 'My Account', quoting your order number (which, of course, you have mislaid) and clicking on a button hidden away out of sight at the bottom of the screen. Should you have a problem, you can always call customer service. But only between nine in the morning and five in the evening (although not at lunchtime and not after three in the afternoon on Fridays). It doesn't exactly exude customer friendliness, does it?

FREITAG also has customer service, in case your bag needs repairing. A box on their website informs you that Dani, Tania and Linda, 'the wordy wizards', are 'old hands in the question-and-answer business, who can definitely help you out'. And if you don't have the time or inclination to send a mail, there are direct line numbers to call each of them.

Is there any reason why the friendly and entertaining FREITAG experience should be confined to a consumer environment? None at all. It can just as easily be applied in a B2B environment.

Whoever sends FREITAG a mail, like I did when requesting photo material for this book, will get an amusing, quick and correct reply in return. Also note in the illustration just how easy it is to contact the company's different divisions.

Figure 2.7 Customer service, the FREITAG way

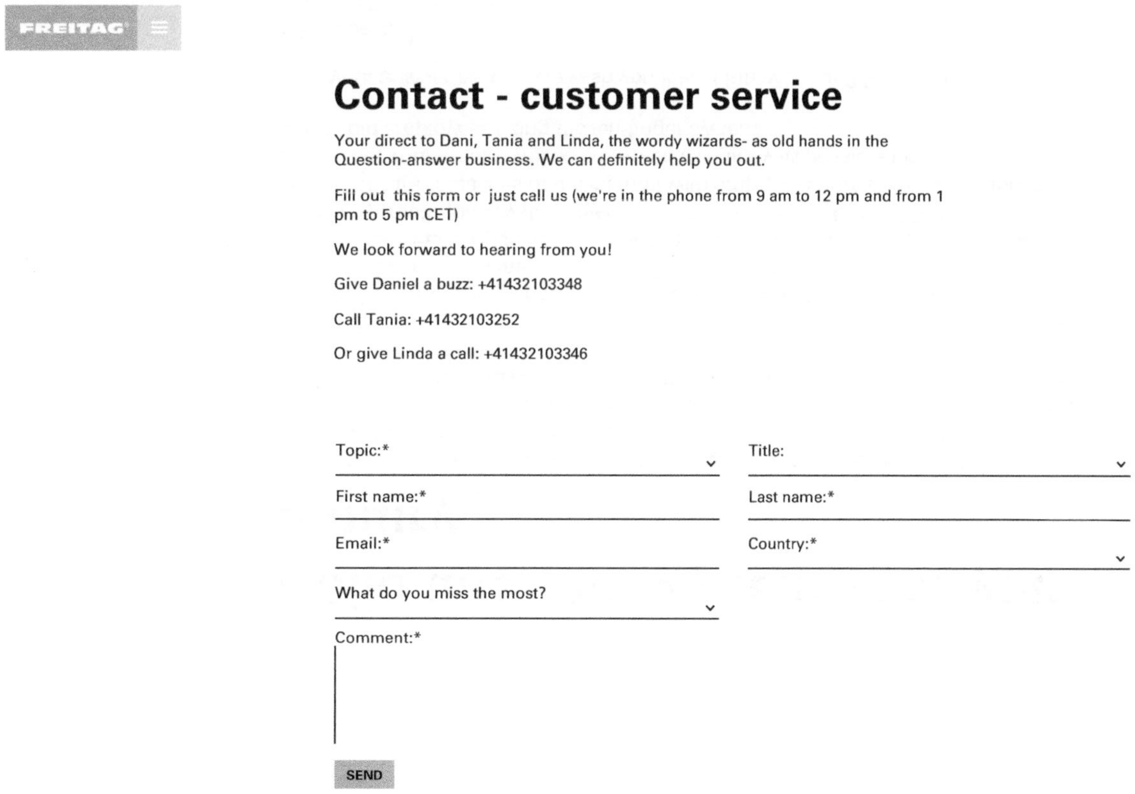

FREITAG

Contact - customer service

Your direct to Dani, Tania and Linda, the wordy wizards- as old hands in the Question-answer business. We can definitely help you out.

Fill out this form or just call us (we're in the phone from 9 am to 12 pm and from 1 pm to 5 pm CET)

We look forward to hearing from you!

Give Daniel a buzz: +41432103348

Call Tania: +41432103252

Or give Linda a call: +41432103346

Topic:*

Title:

First name:*

Last name:*

Email:*

Country:*

What do you miss the most?

Comment:*

SEND

SOURCE ©FREITAG

Figure 2.8 An amusing FREITAG mail in answer to a request

FREITAG° ≡

Hello and many thanks for your inquiry.

Your email has been received, printed and placed in the question pot. Our happy go lucky robot. Ga;SH-i 2016, regularly draws a question from the pot and reads it out to the group gathered round., and then we all use every bit of brainpower we possess to come up with a good answer. We are crossing our fingers that your question will be the next one to be drawn.

Well, to be completely honest, it doesn't quite work that way. Unfortunately, GA;SH-i 2011 was utterly overwhelmed within milliseconds by the task assigned to him because the FREITAG Online Team answers questions at such a rapid pace that the robot's hydraulic joint system overheated, to put it midly. Ga;SH-i 2016 has since left for the far-off reaches of the internet with empty memory banks and dangling cables. So, your inquiry will be answered as quickly as possible by one of our humanoid employees using the ten-finger system.

Until your answer arrives, we wish you lots of fun with our 3.0 website.

All the best,
The FREITAG Online cybogs

SOURCE ©FREITAG

Notes

1 Maes, Patrick (2014) *Turn Opportunity into Sales Results*, CPI-Consulting

2 Walker [accessed August 2015] Customers 2020: A Progress Report [Online] http://www.walkerinfo.com/Customers2020/

3 De Vynck, T and Brodala, Y [accessed Dec 2017] De beste verkoper is geen verkoper, *De Tijd* [Online] http://www.tijd.be/tech-media/media-marketing/De-beste-verkoper-is-geen-verkoper/9551451

4 Warc [accessed May 2017] Customer service gets social in UK [Online] https://www.warc.com/newsandopinion/news/customer_service_gets_social_in_uk/29854

5 Lithium [accessed August 2015] A Community-Driven Culture at giffgaff Drives Competitive Advantage [Online] http://www.lithium.com/why-lithium/customer-success/giffgaff

6 Burn-Callander, R [accessed August 2015] Giffgaff, the 'bonkers' mobile network, proves that the crowd can run your business for you, *The Telegraph* [Online]

7 giffgaff [accessed August 2015] Become a giffgaff Expert [Online] https://experts.giffgaff.com

8 Melis, A [accessed August 2015] Nederlander maakt met dit slimme trucje treintickets goedkoper voor iedereen, *HLN.be* [Online] http://www.hln.be/hln/nl/943/Consument/article/detail/2421994/2015/08/13/Nederlander-maakt-met-dit-slimme-trucje-treintickets-goedkoper-voor-iedereen.dhtml

9 Wever, V [accessed August 2015] NS wil in gesprek met groepsretoursite, *OV Magazine* [Online] http://www.ovmagazine.nl/2015/08/ns-wil-in-gesprek-met-groepsretoursite-1223/

10 Van den Bogaert, R [accessed May 2015] Veranderen of verdwijnen: het autobedrijf van de toekomst, *Vroom.be* [Online] http://www.vroom.be/nl/autonieuws/interview-luc-de-moor-educam-autobedrijf-toekomst

11 Van den Bogaert [accessed May 2015]

PART TWO
There is no excuse for being boring

Creating your value proposition for disruptive selling

03

> The most important thing for the customer is the value you can create for them. This chapter will tell you what this value involves, and how you can manage it throughout the customer journey.

Putting the customer at the centre

Perhaps you have not been unduly worried by what you have read so far, because you have already put the customer at the centre of your business model. And since you have done it already, you see no reason for any further change.

But are you sure? What exactly do you mean by 'putting the customer at the centre'? How can you define it? What does it involve? And does it signify the same thing to everyone in the company? Does it mean the same for the sales department as the marketing department? And what does it mean for the driver who delivers the products? Or the technician who maintains them?

If you are not careful, 'putting the customer at the centre' will be interpreted in many different ways throughout your organization. What's more, it means very little to the customer to hear that they are 'at the centre', unless this idea is translated into coordinated action that creates something of value for them.

For this reason, it is crucial as a first step to define for everyone in the organization precisely what 'at the centre' means in practical terms. What extra value do you want to create? What does this involve? What action or behaviour does this require from your different members of staff?

> Every member of staff needs to understand what 'putting the customer at the centre' means.

Let's talk for a moment in terms of extremes. For one organization, putting the customer at the centre may mean that the customer is always right. At the opposite end of the spectrum, it might mean something like 'raking in as much profit as quickly as we can and adopting an uncompromising attitude when dealing with even the most minor of complaints'.

I believe in the power of happy customers. In the long term, happy customers increase the value of the brand and the company. But if you take things too far in your efforts to create happy customers, there is a danger that you may lose sight of the needs of your own organization. This might make the customer super-happy in the short term, but it is not sustainable in the long term. Catering to the customer's every whim ultimately means becoming their slave! If your customers expect everything as quickly as possible and as cheaply as possible (sometimes even for free), this can only be at the expense of the commercial focus and health of your company.

However, putting the customer at the centre exclusively from the perspective of the company doesn't work either. If you regard customers as a target for easy pickings, you will soon find yourself forced out of the market. Nowadays, unhappy customers are more than ready to tell their horror stories about your company to whoever will listen, and not just on social media. Negative mouth-to-mouth reports spread far more quickly than positive ones, because negative news has a far bigger impact on people – and also attracts far more readers in the press. Having said that, a really strong good news story can still be a powerful tool for brand enhancement.

> Take a balanced approach to putting the customer at the centre, an approach that takes account of the interests of both the customer and the company.

The most sensible option is to take a balanced approach to putting the customer at the centre, an approach that takes account of the interests of both the customer and the company. This implies much more than simply offering the best price or the most favourable conditions. Putting the customer at the centre from the perspective of the company means that you need to develop a value proposition that persuades the customer to pay a fair and correct price. In other words, a price that will allow your company to grow sustainably into the future.

This value proposition must cover the accumulated benefits on which the positioning of the brand is based. Strong and successful brands offer a combination of benefits that provide a clear and consistent picture of the needs that the brand seeks to satisfy. In other words, the value proposition answers the question: 'Why should I buy your brand?'[1]

Developing a value proposition that 'puts the customer at the centre' therefore implies seeking to fulfil the needs which the customer is experiencing in their context at that particular time. This further implies that the same customer can have different needs in other contexts and at other moments in time. The company must be aware of this and respond accordingly.

Imagine that you are the supplier of a scarce raw material. Your customer is highly dependent on your production. Putting customers at the centre could mean that you ask them: 'What do you think is a fair price for my product?' Of course, the laws of supply and demand still apply and it goes without saying that you will attempt to maximize the price. However, you also sell other raw materials and you are keen to expand your brand in the future.

For this reason, it may be wise instead to keep your customer informed about price changes for your scarcest product – or to make it possible to place orders for it 24/7, or to set up a system that allows your most loyal customers to bid first for a particular consignment. Or all three. This will help to develop your business as a whole.

The Kraljic matrix

The matrix devised by Peter Kraljic[2] helps you to assess the strength of your company's position, viewed from the perspective of the customer and, in particular, their purchase strategy. How important are your products and services for the customer? To what extent is the customer strategically dependent, and is there a supply risk? How significant is the financial impact of the products and services on the total value of the products for your customer and on the supply levels in their company?

The Kraljic model has been around for quite some time and helps give shape to an optimized and professional purchasing strategy. What's more, it can be used to draw up a strategy for each individual quadrant in the matrix. And, of course, a sales strategy can also be devised to match each purchasing strategy.

Figure 3.1   The Kraljic matrix

SOURCE Adapted from Kraljic (1983)

The model makes a distinction between four product and service categories.

Strategic products and services
These are high financial impact – that is, essential for the business process or product of the purchaser. Such products have a high supply risk, caused either through scarcity or possible delivery problems, and there are relatively few suppliers in the market.

   As a result, it is the suppliers who take the lead, and the most crucial matter is not so much the price, but the reliability of product availability and the cover of potential price risks. Of course, the large volumes usually involved mean that price remains an important negotiating consideration and the aim is to reach a solution that is acceptable to both parties.

Bottleneck products and services
These are low financial impact and high supply risk. Because the financial impact is low, there is generally minimal price negotiation. Consequently, a company that systematically takes up a bottleneck position in relation to its customers often finds itself in a comfortable position. Above all, it can maximize its price levels with comparative ease.

Leverage products and services
These are high financial impact and low supply risk. This relates to products that consume a significant proportion of the total purchasing budget of the purchaser, but where the purchaser also has a choice of numerous different suppliers in the market, making it easy to switch from one supplier

to another. It also makes it easy for the purchaser to apply pressure to the competing suppliers, allowing them to play off one against the other.

This is a 'red ocean' market. It is not a nice market to work in. You will only survive if your company can repeatedly generate efficiency improvements or devise other benefits that will persuade consumers to opt for you.

Routine (non-critical) products and services

These are low financial impact and low supply risk. This relates to products and services that are readily available and have only a limited influence on company results. In this case, the purchaser will go in search of the best deal, making sure that the price is good, that quality levels are maintained and that ordering/delivery are straightforward.

Once these parameters have been established, suppliers can work relatively undisturbed. Or at least they can until the purchaser's next round of price comparisons, or unless a new disrupter appears on the scene, offering an easier and (usually) cheaper solution that allows the customer to replace the existing supplier quickly and efficiently.

Insights from our own research

CPI frequently conducts research into non-price-related supplier preference drivers. This research has resulted in some interesting insights. For example, in some situations differences of up to 20 per cent between suppliers will be tolerated before serious consideration is given to changing supplier. In other situations, a difference of just a few percentage points is sufficient to prompt supplier change. It all depends on the company's customer portfolio and the other customers who are active in the same sector.

The CPI research has shown that the Kraljic position plays an important role in this. But the purchaser-supplier relationship is also subject to a series of other tangible and intangible factors, whose influence can be equally crucial. In each company it is usually possible to find groups of customers who are motivated by specific value propositions that remain impervious to the effect of other possible factors. Yet at the same time, different groups of customers with the same company regard these other factors – which are of no relevance for the first group – as their key drivers for supplier preference.

Mapping this information and keeping it up to date, so that new customer experiences can be developed to reflect continuing change, is the core of customer-centric selling, which in turn is an essential part of disruptive selling. Many companies make the mistake of stubbornly persisting with a one-size-fits-all value proposition. Instead of satisfying everyone, this constricting uniformity actual satisfies no one, since it is based on general observations rather than the more specific approach that today's markets demand.

Placing the customer in a central position is, above all, a question of offering the customer in a respectful and authentic manner precisely what they need at that particular moment. Working from this basic position and rooted in this basic respect, the objective is to provide an attractive and made-to-measure value proposition.

This value proposition might mean that you enter the market as a price-breaker. However, you will need to make clear to the customer that they must do nearly all the work themselves: monitor their stock, place the orders, collect the goods, provide the transport, complete the necessary paperwork, etc. For some types of customer, this can be a very good value proposition.

At the other end of the scale, you might prefer to offer customers a complete 24/7 service: you monitor their stock, order and store the products you think they need, pack and deliver them just-in-time, using your own transport, etc. This may require you to ask the customer to brainstorm about your product/service and the way that you provide it.

Alternatively, you can involve customers in certain key decisions that affect them. Perhaps it will be necessary – and desirable – to involve the customer in the design of your product or service, perhaps on the basis of a digital menu developed specifically for that purpose. In some cases, it may even be advisable to discuss the pricing of your product or service with your key customers.

At one extreme, you only involve customers to the extent that you provide a product and they pay for it. At the other extreme, you approach every phase of the customer journey with an exaggerated customer orientation. This may even go as far as involving the customer in the design, pricing, delivery and after-service of your product.

The customer journey

The term 'customer journey' means exactly what it says. The relationship with the customer is a shared journey that you make together, where you meet each other along the way at regular intervals. Your aim at each stage must be to persuade the customer to continue their journey further with your company. Throughout this journey, it is the customer who is behind the wheel and makes the decisions.

The relationship with the customer is a shared journey.

A classic metaphor that has been used in recent years to describe the customer journey is the comparison with a funnel. In this funnel approach, it is assumed that potential customers start their journey with a number of products and a number of possible partners in mind.

These options are then systematically reduced in a linear process until the optimum solution – the right product and the right partner – has been found. It is also assumed that the choice of this best possible solution will be influenced by the most assertive (or at least the most active) supplier.

Within the funnel approach, contact with the customer is limited to a series of fixed moments. The customer sees an advertisement, phones for more information, is contacted immediately by a sales rep, is given a costed proposal, signs an order, receives their delivery and pays the invoice.

Sales take the lead. It is the sales function that guides the customer through the purchase process and the sales team will be their only point of contact with the supplier company. As a result, within the funnel approach the commercial organization focuses heavily on the moment immediately prior to the sale. As long as the customer makes a purchase, so that the sales team and individual sales staff can meet their targets, the supplier is happy. This is the key element in the relationship.

Some attention may also be devoted to repeat orders and after-sales care, but these are essentially secondary considerations. The main aim is to achieve a kind of lock-in situation, which restricts the customer's ability to involve other potential partners in matters relating to resupply and maintenance.

In some cases, the supplier may even think that the income they can generate from the after-market is not really worth the effort.[3] As a result, they may prefer to concentrate all their resources on the generation of initial sales. In short, the initial purchase is also the final objective of the sales strategy.

How the customer obtains product information, what the customer does with the products, what the customer thinks about the products once they have been provided and what they tell other people about these products are all matters that do not reach the radar of this kind of supplier. Similarly, they develop no trajectory that can lead the customer towards a new transaction. They simply trust to luck that the customer will display a degree of loyalty.

In fact, once the sale has been completed, there is no real relationship with the customer – except perhaps a highly opportunistic one. The supplier will only make a further effort if the customer badly needs something or if a further quick and easy sale can be made.

Figure 3.2 The traditional funnel approach: from suspect to order

Today, the customer and the company both prefer to make a longer journey, and it is the customer who is leading the way. The opportunities for the customer to gather information and to manipulate both the purchasing decision and service expectations are almost limitless. Their relationship with the product and the company in the modern market has little in common with the linear funnel approach.

During the search process, and also afterwards, the customer can now make a number of lateral detours. These are the things that stimulate opinion. The motor behind these detours is the omnipresent internet, combined with the instant access of mobile communication. As a result, the customer journey no longer follows a straight path, but a winding one.[4]

The customer journey no longer follows a straight path, but a winding one.

Figure 3.3 Customers can adopt an advocacy or a detractor position at any stage in their journey

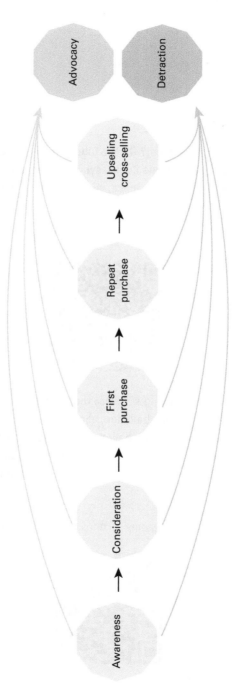

SOURCE ©CPI-Consulting

The customer journey starts when awareness is created. A creative example of building awareness is the Oreo case.

CASE STUDY

Gamification: Oreo Dunk Challenge

Ever heard of an Oreo dunk event? On YouTube you can watch videos of freestyle dunks, long distance dunks, drone dunks, synchronized dunks, star treatment dunks, upside down dunks, drone dunks, mind-reading technology dunks… and it's all about the cookies and glass of milk.

Figure 3.4   QR code: Drone dunk

Oreo also created a mind-reading software that tracks the concentration levels of participants in an Oreo dunk challenge, allowing them to control the cookie by their mind-waves. People were challenged head to head on opposite ends of tables wearing the brain-sensing headbands which would move an Oreo towards them and 'dunk' it into the milk hands-free; the strongest mind to win the competition!

Figure 3.5   QR code: Mind reading technology dunk with Shaquille O'Neal

The customer journey can be divided into four main phases. First, there is the phase in which a purchase is being considered and relevant information is gathered online. This is the phase of *initial consideration*.

Next, there is a phase in which the different alternative solutions are actively investigated. Potential partners are compared and a shortlist of the most likely suppliers is drawn up. This is the phase of *active evaluation*.

The third phase is the phase in which the purchase is actually concluded. A commitment is made. The potential customer becomes an actual customer. This is the *closing*.

Following the purchase, there is a final long phase when the customer uses and experiences what they have bought. This is the *post-purchase* phase, which lasts from the moment when the product is first taken into use until the moment when the product comes to the end of its life cycle and needs to be replaced.

Before the sale, your focus as a supplier is on the possible purchase of your product. After the sale, this focus needs to shift to its possible repurchase, the purchase of additional services and accessories relating to the product, and the active promotion of all these elements. Remember, however, that throughout this process the customer is continually collecting new information, communicating with others and considering decisions. This is why we speak of the *customer decision journey*.

In each of the phases – while considering, evaluating, purchasing and using – the customer is constantly developing their thinking and reaching new conclusions. Each phase also provides opportunities for a number of contact moments. Within this loop, the customer searches for information in very different ways, and also analyses and assesses it in very different ways.

They are looking to find a new role in their relationship with the potential supplier. If they succeed, the customer will ultimately communicate their experience of the purchased product to others and even try to influence their opinion about it.

A straightforward list of the number of visits to your website does not give you enough information to trace and follow up possible leads in a targeted manner. Yet this is what you need to do if you want to manage and grow a customer relationship. Tracking modern consumers in the various twists and turns they make can no longer be done with a simple Excel file in which past interests and questions are recorded. Nowadays, this increasingly complex task needs to be carried out by marketing automation tools and customer engagement software.

It is simply impossible for a human being to trace a visit to a website and decipher the intentions concealed within the visitor's online behaviour.

Figure 3.6 The Get-Grow funnel

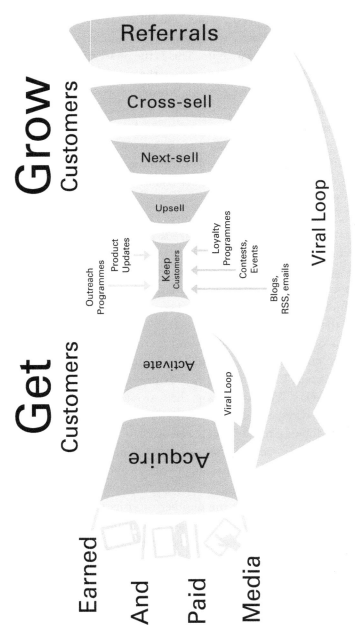

SOURCE Steve Blank

No one can look inside the internet, never mind collect, collate, categorize and analyse the digital body language, search tasks and online communication of (potential) customers. And this is before we even mention the need to combine these analyses and convert them into usable metrics for developing appropriate actions at the right time with the right content.

Marketing automation and its associated software can do all these things. And all in real time.

---

85 per cent of online visitors are just 'looking around'

85 per cent of the people who visit your website and spend a minute of their time there do not necessarily plan to buy one of your products.[5] They are just interested. Browsing. Looking around.

If you start to stalk everyone who visits your site, bombarding them with mails and telephone calls, you are going against the current trend that gives the customer the lead role in the sales story.

CASE STUDY

The Barcelona Street Project, easyjet

When you think about booking a flight to Barcelona, the standard customer journey that comes to mind might start with an online comparison of airline offerings, prices and time schedules, all seasoned with the emotion of past experiences in relation to this or that airline. You make your choice, confirm the dates, fill in the identity forms, transfer the money and print your ticket.

A few days before the flight, you check in on the airline's website and print your boarding pass. The next contact point is when you get to the airport, drop off your bags, spend some checking and queuing time and board the plane. Subsequently the plane takes off and you hope for a smooth landing, accompanied by some refreshments and attentive on-board personnel.

Once safely on the tarmac, you hope you can efficiently disembark and walk out of the airport with all your belongings, before making your way to Las Ramblas in Barcelona and trusting your phone to guide you via Google Maps.

easyJet stretched the customer journey by making it easier to get around when you explore your city of destination.

easyJet took this airline customer journey to the next level, not by offering an extra pre-boarding or on-board service, but by stretching the journey itself and making it easier to get around when you explore your city of destination. They introduced the easyJet Sneakairs, vibrating smart shoes which come with sensors connected to a smartphone app via Bluetooth.[6] You program a sightseeing tour using the app and the shoes will vibrate you to your destination, providing you with hands-free directions.

The system uses GPS to track your location. When approaching an intersection and depending on the required direction, it sends a vibration to the appropriate foot, indicating you to make a left or right turn. Two consecutive vibrations on both shoes mean you've overshot the required street or made a wrong turn. Three vibrations indicate that you have arrived at your destination.[7]

Why bother, you might think. You have an active map in your pocket: your phone shows the way. Well, first of all it might be easier to walk the streets without having to refer to a map or a phone for directions. Second, you don't show off your expensive mobile gear in plain sight, making you a smaller target for gizmo thieves, although you might be tempted to use your mobile screen to scroll information when enjoying the sights you encounter. And third, you look less like an intrusive tourist on the verge of getting lost – although bright orange sneakers may not necessarily improve your camouflage.

The Sneakairs were tested at easyJet's 'Barcelona Street Project' event. easyJet is seriously considering the further development as an item ready available to purchase for passengers on-board its flights.

Figure 3.7   QR code: The Barcelona Street Project

Personae

A classic (and, in the past, a reasonably effective) way to divide customers into categories is to make use of objective criteria, such as age, gender and location. These criteria also have the advantage of being easy to ascribe.

But if you want to develop a commercial approach in which the customer is central, you need to do something more.

The complexities of customer behaviour – how the customer thinks, what they feel and how they will react throughout the customer journey – cannot be understood within the stereotypical and restrictive context of 'male/female', 'younger than 25/older than 60' and 'lives in Brussels/London'.

It is much more useful to identify the number of different archetypes within your portfolio of (potential) customers. These archetypes are usually referred to as *personae* and they can be identified through target group research that investigates how different types of people react to your product.

You can start with a very simple classification; for example, 'easy' and 'difficult' customers. Who are they? How does their behaviour differ? What are their preferences? What are their different needs? What do they like and dislike? On the basis of the results, it will usually be possible to draw up a number of clearly defined personality types. You can even give these a name and a face, so that you can quite literally visualize each different customer type.

Each type can also be linked to a customer profile, which details likely expectations, behaviour, stress factors and happiness factors. These profiles should be spread throughout the entire organization: it is important that everyone is singing from the same hymn sheet.

I know of companies where the different personae are explicitly depicted in promotional material, such as pamphlets, posters and even dummies dressed in shop windows. Often, they are given names just like real customers. Fred. Frankie. Sebastian. Jean-Claude. Emily.

If discussion arises within the company about the development of a product or the roll-out of a marketing action, it is always possible to ask: 'How would Jean-Claude react to this message?' or 'How would Emily like to see this product?'

Personae make it possible to better appreciate, almost take part in, the lives of these realistic but fictitious customer personalities.[8] The intention is that they should each represent a particular customer segment, for each of which a typical customer journey should be mapped out. What are their information-gathering preferences? At what moments do they need that information? How will they find you? Do they use social media? Do they respond to paid advertising?

Each type will experience the different phases of the purchase process in a different way. It is important that you have a clear picture of these expected patterns of experience. This will help you, for example, to decide which types of questions you ask each type of customer. Unless you interact with each different persona in a different way, you will not achieve the results you desire.

Create different personae and map out a typical customer journey for
each of them.

The personae must remain realistic and usable for everyone in the organization. They serve as an instrument to gain insight into customer behaviour
and are not an end in themselves. It is standard practice to develop just three
or four personae, with five as an absolute maximum.

Another possible way to deal with wide-ranging customer expectations and desires is to offer a number of well-targeted basic variants
of your product. Customers can then further develop and equip these
variants in the manner that best suits their own circumstances. You
give them a basic platform and some building blocks, so that they can
make their own made-to-measure product. This is a technique that has
been successfully applied by Apple: customers buy the type of iPhone
or iPad they think they need, and then add the apps and accessories
they most want.

Initial consideration

During the period when the potential customer is still considering whether
to make a purchase or not, they are influenced by impulses from a wide variety of different sources. These include the media, visits to trade fairs, stories
from colleagues, posts that they come across online, etc.[9]

In this way, a number of brands and messages will become subcon-
sciously embedded in the customer's mind; brands and messages to which
they become attached. When the moment arrives that the potential customer
decides to move on to the more active investigation of the possible purchase,
they will first focus their efforts on the brands and messages that are already
clearly lodged in their head.

Potential customers usually have the tendency to keep their first list of
potential suppliers fairly short. They have heard about a particular product
and are considering its purchase. But they are most likely to start their investigations with a brand that they know or have heard/read about. To make
sure that your brand finds its way onto this initial shortlist, you first need to
make sure that it is recognized and remembered by the customer. Brands that
succeed in doing this are 300 per cent more likely to be purchased than other
brands.[10]

Being included in this first shortlist is therefore a major advantage. But
failure to achieve this does not mean that all is lost. In contrast to the linear
funnel concept, where the potential customer systematically scraps one brand

after another from their list, today's customer compares their original choices with the many interesting alternative offers available online. As a result, new names can also be added as well as old ones crossed off.

Eight seconds, no longer

Digital and mobile consumption, an excess of impulses and information that needs to be reduced to 140 characters all mean that our attention span is getting shorter and shorter. In fact, the average person finds it hard to concentrate on something for longer than eight seconds.[11]

This was the startling conclusion of a study commissioned by Microsoft Canada. Put simply, the typical modern, digitally connected person loses concentration more quickly than a goldfish, which has an attention span of nine seconds! Fifteen years ago, before we all became so dependent on our smartphones and the internet, the average human attention span was 12 seconds.[12] In other words, our ability to concentrate has deteriorated by a third.

What's more, this eight seconds has nothing to do with the length of time that people are prepared to wait for access to an internet page. This waiting time is just a paltry two seconds; if they have to wait three seconds, around 40 per cent of visitors immediately leave the site.[13] Even if you can keep them, you only have a maximum of four seconds to attract and hold their attention for the core of your message. During this first four seconds, you must make sufficient impact to earn their attention for the remaining four seconds of their concentration time.

Roughly 17 per cent of all web pages are viewed for less than four seconds. Only 4 per cent are viewed for more than a couple of minutes.[14]

Of course, the results of the Canadian study do not mean that people are never able to focus on anything for longer than eight seconds. If something excites our interest, we can concentrate on it for much longer periods. Eight seconds is the time we allow for that initial interest to be stimulated. And if this brief window is likely to become smaller and smaller in the future (which seems probable), this is something that online marketers will need to take into account.

This is already the case with television advertising. The average TV commercial lasts between 15 and 30 seconds, but the makers know that the real impact needs to be made during the first four seconds; otherwise, the viewers' attention will start to wander. If the attention is captured and held, only then can the remaining seconds be used to get additional information across.

Children spend many hours on YouTube and other platforms, where the use of advertising is generally experienced as something irritating. The clever sites try to get around this with equally clever games. Think, for example, of YouTube, where you try to close your eyes for the length of the advert before each clip, and then click at the exact moment when you think it has finished.

If you watch television almost any evening, you will soon see that some advertisers have not yet learnt these basic lessons. Advertising needs to be inspirational *and* entertaining. Testimonials, summaries of product benefits and company messages are nearly always experienced by viewers as being inappropriate or unwelcome. If they want extra information, they can do so later at a time of their own choosing.

This helps to explain the success of ad blockers and the huge lack of sympathy for the publishers who want to restrict their use. Put simply, people hate bad and boring adverts. But the opposite is also true. Good advertising, original spots and ingenious promotional games are all incredibly popular, particularly with young people, who view and share them over and over again.

Active evaluation

In the past, customers tended to select a limited number of brands and products, from which they would then make their final choice. Today's customers prefer to keep an open mind, subjecting their shortlist to detailed scrutiny and adding new brands or products that they may discover during the investigative process. In other words, the active evaluation of brands and products is much longer and more thorough than it used to be.

Naturally, this is the result of the huge amount of information that is now available to consumers. This wealth of data allows customers to continuously alter their selection criteria. The internet offers hundreds of potential solutions. To find them, all the customer needs to do is click from one website to another. This can lead to a degree of indecision or the need for yet more research, which further lengthens this phase of the purchasing process.

This is the moment at which the marketeers can enter the process, by developing appropriate activities and content. Your marketing must ensure that you only offer smart information – and only for as long as the customer feels that this extra knowledge adds something to their ability to make the best choice. It is important to avoid information overload, so that the customer can no longer see the wood for the trees. This will lead to doubt. It is the brand's task to remove this doubt by showing that it properly understands the customer's needs. This is essential, if the customer is to finally decide in your favour.

In part, this overload is the customer's own fault, because they have taken so much of the modern sales story on their own shoulders. They inevitably come into contact with huge amounts of information, either actively or passively. Wise companies avoid making this problem worse by bombarding the customer with mails and promo material.

What really helps is to show customers that your organization is the best partner to guide them through their customer journey. This will not only allow you to persuade the customer to add your product to their shortlist, but might also ensure that some of your rivals are crossed off. Of course, this also means that if you were fortunate enough to be on the original list, your place is not necessarily secure. Other companies will be trying to do the same to you!

The power of the publicity you earn (the comments of satisfied customers or the opinions of independent trendsetters) is much greater than the publicity you own (your website and social media channels) or the publicity you pay for (advertisements, banners, sponsored content, etc).

This is where you can see the power of the loop. One of your customers will always be better able than you to persuade another customer. This is the reason why it is so important to maintain good relations with your customers in the after-sale period. It encourages them to purchase accessories (or make repeat purchases), and may even prompt them to tell others just how satisfied they are with your products and your relationship. As the old marketing adage puts it: free publicity is the best publicity. And nowhere is this truer than with word-of-mouth.

Post-purchase

Customers continue to consider and reconsider their options until they finally come to a decision and make a purchase. From the moment this purchase has been made, the customer's user experience begins. This means that they will assess the value that you promised them. They evaluate whether the product lives up to the expectations that you helped to create before the sale. Delivery time: check. User-friendliness: check. Production capacity: check. Energy consumption: check. Ease of maintenance: check. And so on. Everything that you said to promote your product will be tested against the reality of its experience.

Even after the purchase is completed, many customers continue to search for information about unknown product characteristics, other applications, accessories, other people's experiences, etc. If their experience matches up to their prior expectations, there is a chance that these customers will pass on their opinions to others, perhaps even becoming brand ambassadors. However, if customers find that they have been sold short, not only will they make difficulties but also communicate their frustration to anyone who will listen.

It is therefore critical to keep customers as satisfied as possible, so that they remain within the loop of their loyalty circle. If every experience during each contact moment is positive, the customer will also continue to identify positively with your product. As a result, within the same circle they will return to your company whenever they want to buy the same or similar products, and will recommend to peers to do the same.

The need for excellent after-sales service is nothing new. However, there are different ways that you can work with loyal customers. In short, they can either be actively or passively loyal. Customers who are passively loyal stay with your brand because they are used to it. It is their easiest option. But they do not see it as a love brand. Consequently, they will make no effort to promote it. On the contrary, they may be open to interesting overtures from your rivals.

Customers who are actively loyal have confidence in your brand, are emotionally attached to it and willing to promote it. It is on this group that you need to focus your attention. Your aim must be to develop ordinary customers into loyal customers, and loyal customers into ambassadors.

Thanks to marketing automation, it is now also possible to better follow up the after-sales trajectory of your customers, so that you can respond to their specific needs at precisely the right moment. A screening and analysis of their online traffic should quickly tell you whether a customer is actively or passively loyal. And if your products are smart, so that they transmit data about their own use, you can use this information to even further refine your customer profile.

Social trackers

It has recently become popular to depict the modern customer journey as a cloud. This reflects the ability of customers in our hyper-connected and online-networked world to change their opinion at any moment. There is always a new opportunity, a new possibility, a new tool, new information, a new trigger or a new opinion. At any moment, the customer can, if they so wish, switch from being an ambassador to a detractor.

This bipolarity means that customer loyalty is a very fickle thing. It can be given and taken away in the blink of an eye. For me, this cloud thinking is yet another reason for focusing on marketing automation. Why? Because it allows your organization to follow the moment, to be part of it. This is the only way to keep abreast of the real needs of the customer at every point of contact.

With this in mind, it is very important to listen to what is happening on social media via social trackers, such as Obi4Wan and Radion6. These trackers trawl social media channels in search of posts in which your brand, company or any other selected search term are mentioned. In this way, millions of posts can be monitored each second. If there is a match, your social media desk will be sent a copy of the post. In some cases, there is literally a flashing red light! Whether the post is good or bad, you are at least aware of what it says and can respond, if appropriate.

Nowadays, reputations are made and broken online. If you don't know what people are saying about you on the web, your company is running blind. One of the examples I like to discuss in my training sessions is the unfortunate experience of a major flour supplier. Circumstances dictated that the supplier felt obliged to increase their price to their customers. However, the communication of this decision was made via an impersonal letter.

To make matters worse, it was sent during the holiday period. This was contractually correct, but the bakers reacted furiously. Depending on the severity of the reaction, the supplier began to make concessions on a case by case basis. Several clever bakers started a Facebook group. It is not difficult to guess the outcome. The bakers began to exchange details of the prices they had been able to negotiate, which resulted in a negative price spiral for the supplier in their further dealings with other bakers.

It was not long before the supplier became aware of the Facebook group's existence. At first, they were furious, but they soon began to realize that they had handled the situation badly. The moral of the story? The supplier now understands that social media needs to be followed – and followed closely. They have even appointed a social media marketeer – and a new commercial director.

The secret of sales success in the modern marketplace is to quickly track down viral stories involving your company, so that you can react with equal speed. It is also useful to search for online stories in which you can play a role. My Antwerp colleague once had a problem with the services of the internet provider Telenet. He was angry because on his first free evening for months he was unable to watch the film of his choice. To vent his frustration, he placed this photo on Facebook.

Figure 3.8 OBI4WAN, one of the best performing social trackers on the market

SOURCE Obi4Wan

Figure 3.9 Telenet's exemplary customer service

The reaction of Telenet was immediate and flawless.

So, too, was the feedback from my colleague. A satisfied customer can help to support the image of Telenet (or any other company) as a rapidly reacting and customer-friendly organization. This is a good example of how customers are finding the use of trackers increasingly normal, since more and more of them are experiencing that it can also result in benefits for them.

It is certainly the case that many target groups now expect that each and every question they pose (or criticism they make) will be dealt with quickly and automatically – and often with a reward. For example, anyone who has a problem with the drive belt on their washing machine no longer bothers to call customer service, but instead places an amusing post and photo online. They rightly expect that this will be picked up by the company's tracker and dealt with promptly.

And this is indeed what usually happens – at least with forward-thinking companies who have invested in the right technology. Having said that, there are still many companies who fail to live up to their customers' expectations on social media.

This was the conclusion of a survey of consumers by the Northridge Group in the US.[15] A third of the consumers who had asked a question or reported a problem online never received an answer from the company concerned. And this even though many consumers only post messages when the problem is getting out of hand. Nevertheless, 47 per cent of the consumers questioned said that in the years ahead they intend to use social media just as much or even more for dealing with their customer service issues.

Morton's steak at the airport

Venture capitalist Peter Shankman was hungry when he boarded his flight to Newark in the US. He sent a tweet to Morton's Steakhouse, asking them if they could meet him with a steak at the airport when he landed just two hours later. Morton's duly obliged!

The story of the Morton steak is a classic example of how to listen and react to what is being said about you on social media. It also demonstrates how easy it can be to get valuable media attention for your brand and your customer-friendliness at no cost. Today, this is how companies create *customer delight* – a concept that in the years ahead will become commonplace.

For the record, Shankman has 100,000 followers on Twitter and is a regular customer at Morton's. And the story about his tweet is not new: it already dates from 2011.[16] The stunt not only gave Morton's Steakhouse priceless free publicity in their home market. It also provided international exposure on a previously unprecedented scale.

As a result, many international travellers decided to give their steakhouse a try during their next visit to the US. Earned content on a worldwide scale. Just count that profit!

Figure 3.10   Peter Shankman's tweets to Morton's Steakhouse

@petershankman
Peter Shankman

Hey @Mortons - can you meet me at newark airport with a porterhouse when I land in two hours? K, thanks. :)

17 Aug via TwidroydPRO   Favorite   Retweet   Reply

@petershankman
Peter Shankman

Oh. My. God. I don't believe it. @mortons showed up at EWR WITH A PORTERHOUSE! lockerz.com/s/130578715 # OMFG!

Contact strategy

Every experience during every contact moment with a customer has the potential to trigger a decision that will determine their behaviour in a following phase of the customer journey. It is therefore important to know which contact moments are highly relevant to the customer – and can make a difference – and also what they expect from you at such moments. Once you know this, you can make these contact moments more valuable for the customer – and for your company.

If a customer wants information, they will almost certainly turn to the internet, visiting the websites of potential suppliers and gathering together the data that they think is relevant to their situation. The website is therefore the pre-eminent means of establishing first contact with potential customers. And this first contact needs to make its mark immediately. The customer is expecting more than 'just some information'. They are expecting the information that they need at that particular point in the customer journey.

What's more, they expect it in a language they can understand and in a form that will allow them to move forward to the next phase of their journey. As if this were not enough, they also expect immediate and 24/7 access to this information. For all these reasons, the use of dynamic content in websites is crucial. I will tell you how you can do this later in the book.

Customers decide for themselves when they are ready to further investigate and make concrete their intentions. When they contact your company, you can reasonably assume that they have already been in detailed contact with other potential suppliers. If the customer just asks for more information, give it without trying to immediately push them in the direction of a purchase. You can certainly suggest (gently!) a series of possible next steps and perhaps even an action or two, but no more than that. The wheeler-dealer days of selling ice to the Eskimos are long gone!

Customers also have similarly high expectations after a purchase has been made. If the product is damaged or defective, or if there is some other problem, they demand an immediate solution or a prompt replacement.

The end of selling ice to the Eskimos

The customer's voyage of discovery to find the perfect solution will involve numerous moments of contact with your company and your competitors. If you can detect and actively influence these moments, you will gain an advantage over your rivals in the race to secure the final purchase. How can you make these contact moments more valuable? What approach should you take? What information should you exchange? What is the competition doing and what response can you expect from them?

You don't always need to wait until the customer takes the initiative to talk to your company. You can also initiate contact moments. If you have collected relevant information of importance or interest for the customer, you can inform them in a carefully compiled (not too pushy!) mail or phone call. It helps, of course, if the content is also present in the fora that the customer consults during their customer journey.

Of course, it is not just about contact moments made directly with your company. For a fee, the sellers of advertising space on the internet will be happy to tell you which potential customers are searching for particular products or services and which of your rivals' website they have already viewed. This gives you the opportunity to proactively contact these potential customers with appropriate messages via diverse media.

In the B2B environment, more and more ideas are being developed that will allow companies to collect and distil information from social media for the purpose of selling this information on in the form of leads.

One such company is Datanyze, which has cleverly exploited the fact that the marketing automation of a website is linked to the use of specific codes, which can be identified and deciphered with the right software. Datanyze uses this insight to tell companies in marketing automation which other companies have installed marketing automation on their sites. Most marketing automation projects start with a free trial. This means that everyone can discover that company X is interested in marketing automation and is currently testing the system of company Y. This is the signal for other companies to try and persuade this sales-ready prospect to try out another system before making a final purchase decision.

Targets and sustainability

Having a loyalty loop is all well and good, but how do you combine it with improved sales results? At the end of the day, your business is still about making a profit. And this means more sales.

The pressure to achieve results is ever-present. Yet at the same time you need to cosset the customer at a pace that they set and in a manner that they determine. These are the stresses and strains that commercial organizations need to be able to cope with. Even so, you must avoid the 'sign now otherwise I won't make my quarterly figures and get my bonus' approach. That is the kind of attitude that gave sales such a bad name in recent decades. The aggressive tactics that were once used on customers to achieve targets are no longer compatible with the prevailing customer culture.

Nowadays, if you want to sell more you have to be far less sales-oriented than in the past. Push too hard and your customer will go elsewhere.

The aggressive tactics that were once used on customers to achieve targets are no longer compatible with the prevailing customer culture.

Learn from Salesforce and their realigned sales approach

Marketing automation gives you real-time insight into your customer relationship or into the relationship you are building with a potential customer. But the fact that you are now using marketing automation does not mean that you will no longer make mistakes. One of the main failings of die-hard sellers is that they want to close the deal as soon as the very first purchase signal is received from a prospect. They charge in like a bull at a gate, so that they often frighten off their prey.

For example, Salesforce is a fantastic company with fantastic products in cloud software. Founded in 1999 by Marc Benioff and Parker Harris, it is now one of the world's top ten IT companies. When Salesforce was launched on the stock market in 2004, it had just 400 employees. Today it has 13,000, generating a turnover of 5 billion US dollars between 2010 and 2014. The company was chosen as most innovative company for four successive years by the prestigious *Forbes* magazine.[17]

If you compare all the various CRM systems on the market, the Salesforce system is clearly the best in terms of quality and their website is a model of how you can support customers and keep them informed about the latest technological developments.

However, their success has been a result of moving forward from a 'sales bombardment' mentality and the common sales approach of pulling cold call details from LinkedIn profiles and pushing hard for results. This has improved both their reputation and results immeasurably by realigning to a more consultative approach.

Whoever operates online will automatically have more opportunities to maintain relationships with a wider network of people. All the standard online instruments are useful for this purpose: emails, online advertisements, social media, online videos, etc.

In short, anything that can be used to package content and deliver value to the customer in the right form and at the right moment. Customers are also expecting more instant contact. When they want something, they want it now – and the supplier has to find it, quickly, easily and without problems.

Building an online relationship is like building a physical relationship. First, there is the sniffing phase. Then there is the exploratory phase. Next comes the evaluation phase, when the purchase criteria are carefully weighed up. Finally, the choice is made. This all tends to run fairly smoothly, as long as both parties treat each other with respect and as long as the relationship remains mutually beneficial.

And just like you probably try to avoid people who constantly talk about themselves, so prospects will try to avoid the die-hard sellers who are only interested in repeatedly singing the praises of their own products.

The 4-1-1 rule of social selling

If you make use of social media to start and build your relationship with new prospects, you need to be aware of the benefits of the 4-1-1 rule.[18] This rule was developed by Tippingpoint Labs and Joe Pulizzi, the godfather of content marketing and the founder of the Content Marketing Institute.

The 4-1-1 rule states that you should only start promoting your own offer after you have first re-tweeted one relevant tweet and, more importantly, shared four pieces of relevant content written by others.

Social marketing is therefore a question of first trawling the net to see what other external messages can be shared to support your own message, rather than simply launching your own message on your unprepared prospects from the outset.

Loyalty and sustainability are closely linked to each other. The secret of a sustainable relationship is starting in good time. You need to do everything you can to appear on the customer radar at the earliest possible moment. By providing correct information in a correct and discreet manner to (potential) customers at a very early stage in their customer journey, they will get to know you and come to see you as a possible partner for that journey.

But to achieve this you must be permanently accessible and must also constantly register and reinterpret new data relevant to your relationship. If the customer requests it, provide them with specific, accurate and up-to-date feedback – and do it quickly. Guiding someone on a journey is much more than just wanting to sell them something.

A sustainable relationship and putting the customer under pressure are not compatible.

If the (potential) customers gradually become charmed by the information you are providing, so that they gradually move towards a purchase, there is a very good chance that they will involve you in the evaluation phase. During this phase, they will also recall their previous (positive) experiences. You need to be patient and accept that they may postpone their decision, perhaps because they want to look further at what is on offer online or want to secure the buy-in of colleagues.

But at the moment when the purchase decision is finally taken, the customer will want immediate action. Their cautious approach so far will be replaced by instant expectation. If you succeed in responding to that expectation in a correct manner, you are on the road to building a sustainable relationship.

A sustainable customer relationship means having respect for the customer but also implies that your own shareholders can have respect for your commercial approach. Perhaps today's profit is made less quickly than in the past, but it is probably more sustainable. And by sustainable, I mean successful in the long term.

The customer does the work

Offering value to customers is something very different from reaching your own targets. In the modern market, you need to offer value that sells itself, because it is what the customer wants.

Customers compare products before making a purchase. Even after the purchase, they continue to compare experiences. Whether the customer buys your product and then continues to advertise it no longer depends exclusively on the quality of the product. Nowadays, it also depends on the way you involve the customer in the process and on the level of service you give.

Essentially, customers have become shoppers. They now adopt the behaviour they have learnt as ordinary consumers. If they are not satisfied, they go somewhere better. Your task is to make sure that you can hold their attention and their interest.

The advantage of customers and prospects who seek to inform themselves better than ever before is that they will more easily come into contact with your value proposition. If you inform the customer correctly and relevantly from an early stage, their search for the right product will work to your advantage. In essence, today's customers and prospects find their own way to your company, rather than you finding them. This saves you work. All you need to do is make sure you have put up the right sign-posts along the way.

Modern customers have become empowered, but in exchange they have agreed to take over many of the tasks that were previously expected of suppliers. Successful companies make skilful use of the curiosity and enthu-siasm of these interested customers and prospects. These are the men and women who trawl the internet and social media almost continually, so that they have appropriated large parts of the traditional sales process for them-selves. Quite literally.

All the information that a customer gives to you in the course of their search for the right product is information that you no longer need to find for yourself. The details that the customer leaves behind by ticking boxes and filling in forms online are details that you no longer need to enter into your system. Instead, you can immediately analyse and interpret this wealth of data, which allows you to provide solutions that interest the customer even more.

Having said that, this new kind of commercial openness requires a change of mental attitude, which is reflected in a less overtly commercial approach.

But being more distant and more reserved in your approach does not mean being absent. It means that you follow the customer's journey, help-ing where you can, but not dictating where they should go in a pushy or intrusive manner. You must first give value before you can expect to receive it back. This involves a considerable degree of permission marketing: you only do things with the agreement of the customer. If a customer has been on your radar for quite some time, you can certainly send them two or three enquiry mails, but no more. Stalking customers on the phone after their first visit to your website is also counterproductive.

For companies used to the 'hard-sell' culture of the past, this switch can often be a difficult one to make. Old habits die hard. It is not uncommon for old-style sales managers to demand a list of website visitors from their marketing colleagues. Armed with this list, they systematically contact these visitors by phone, usually in the hope of persuading them to agree to a meet-ing, because meetings lead to sales, don't they?

Maybe in the past, but not anymore. Nowadays, this type of assertive approach will lose your company all credibility with potential customers, with inevitable effects on sales motivation and return.

Being reserved in your approach means letting the customer make the choices on the basis of correct, up-to-date and transparent information. Treat your customer like a partner with whom you wish to establish an authentic and respectful relationship. You can assume that every decision the customer makes of their own free will – from product choice to service levels – is a conscious and well-considered decision. This saves you a huge amount of work in trying to find out exactly what the customer wants, and allows you to formulate a value proposition that you can be confident will meet their expectations.

If customers take the lead in the sales process, if they get exactly what they want at every step of the customer journey, if they can count on your understanding and your willingness to listen, if your input into their journey is both efficient and inspirational, then it is reasonable to assume that they will be happy. Happy customers mean profits. More importantly, happiness also the key to developing loyal customers, who in turn can become ambassadors. And ambassadors are worth their weight in gold in modern markets.

Deliver the goods

Deliver the goods. Do what you promise. Whether we are talking about information, a product or a service, this can make all the difference because a professional relationship is based more on rational considerations than on sympathy, the moral expectation inherent in that relationship is also translated in relational terms, through a signed contract or an order form on paper. And when the delivery is made, it will be checked against the contract or order form to make sure that you have done what you said you would do.

Putting things down on paper is easy if everything is tangible, if it can be sorted and counted, neatly packed in boxes, loaded, transported, unloaded, unpacked and stored. This was possible, as long as a product or service was just a product or service, and nothing more.

But in the modern market, success also depends on your providing other, less tangible benefits. These are much more difficult to quantify. For example, just placing a telephone number on your website does not mean that you are always accessible for your customer.

And it gets even harder when you need to make promises relating to matters like a sales experience, user-friendliness, speed, ease, a particular kind of environment, etc. If you promise to make things easy for the customer, they will decide for themselves precisely what this involves. Nowadays, customers expect companies to be aware of their preferences. They know that companies collect and process online details, notwithstanding the negative privacy implications this can sometimes have. In return for tolerating all this tracking and tracing, the customers expect an optimum service:

'What, you mean you don't send an SMS before you deliver? Surely you know how professionally busy I am! You don't? What's the matter with you? Haven't you got LinkedIn?'

'You know that I ski, because I recently posted a holiday photo on Facebook. So why haven't you amended my insurance policy? You mean you never look at Facebook? What century are you living in?'

'Bunch of amateurs! You need to read a book about disruptive selling!'

And so it goes on. More than you think, and often with more emotion and colourful language!

Customers expect proactive communication and feel cheated if they don't get it. In the era of social media, failure to communicate instantly and accurately is like striking a match in a fireworks factory. It explodes in your face. Worse, it is regarded as bad service. And there is nothing so unpredictable and vengeful as a customer who thinks they have been badly treated.

In broad terms, there are five main reasons for customer dissatisfaction:

1 You promise too much, but deliver less.

2 You fail to communicate proactively.

3 Your service provision does not match up to current coolness standards.

4 You miss customer signals in channels you fail to monitor.

5 You irritate customers by taking decisions instead of giving them the choice or at least consulting them.

As a company, you need to have clear positioning. Once you have decided on your position, it is essential to communicate this clearly to the market. If your value proposition consists of non-innovative products that you promise to sell at the cheapest price, you need to make good this promise. If you do, you will be assessed less critically in other areas. If you promise to be the most innovative, or to provide the best service, but it turns out that you are less creative or customer friendly than you thought, you will have a serious credibility problem.

It is also important to remember that what you promise is not always what your customer will expect on the basis of that promise. The same words have different meanings for different customers – certainly when it comes to the experience aspects of the customer journey.

Your company needs to change with the times. This means that the emphasis in your value proposition will also change. But have you adjusted your website and baseline to reflect this? If not, you are simply helping to create misunderstanding. New and existing customers expect to receive products and services as they are described on your website and promoted in your communication.

The telephonist manning your 0800 line might have a different interpretation about an aspect of your message to their colleague at the next desk, or their manager, or even yourself. What is the maximum number of times the phone can ring? Five times? So do we let the telephone ring five times before we pick it up or do we pick it up on the first ring? And how quick is quick when it comes to making price quotations or passing on orders?

The more explicitly you can communicate these things throughout the entire organization, the better you will be able to provide the kind of uniform experience that customers are seeking.

When it comes to creating value and delivering promises, the CEO plays a crucial role. They need to communicate at all levels of the organization – from top to bottom, both horizontally and vertically – precisely what the company stands for, what it is offering to customers and under what conditions. Like all good communication, this needs to be tailored to specific target groups, both in terms of form and content. The way you communicate your message to your accountant will be different in emphasis and tone from the way you communicate that same basic message to one of your fork-lift drivers.

The important thing is that everyone is on the same wavelength. For example, it frequently happens that pricing policy is amended without the people in marketing and customer service being made aware of this vital information. It is also common for the people in sales to move heaven and earth to win an order, but without passing on this important news to colleagues in other departments.

Delivering a promise is something that involves everyone in the company. The only way to provide a uniform customer experience is to ensure that everyone is singing from the same hymn sheet. And the automation of your processes does not remove the need for good and clear communication from person to person.

Value debundling

You stand on one side of the purchase process, making a promise that you intend to keep. On the other side stands the customer, who expects that what you promise (and provide) will be precisely what is wanted. In other words, customers demand a made-to-measure value proposition and is prepared to pay a price for things that have value for them. Things that have no value for them are worthless in their eyes.

In short, the purchase process is not simply about your company making a promise and keeping it. It is also about providing precisely the value that is most important to the customer at that particular moment in time. Many companies focus too much on keeping their promise, without really knowing (or caring) whether the value inherent in this promise is actually the value that the customer is expecting or most needs. And you will never be able to find this out unless you question the customer on this key matter.

> Many companies focus too much on keeping their promise, without really knowing whether the value inherent in this promise is actually the value that the customer most needs.

It is possible that the customer will be satisfied with what you do throughout the customer journey and will attach great importance to it. But it is equally possible that the customer will be satisfied with what you do throughout the customer journey and attach no importance to it whatsoever.

This type of situation – where you impress customers without actually giving them what they want – is simply throwing away money. When this happens, you need to think again about your approach. Even more damaging are the situations where you offer customers something they value highly, but they remain wholly unsatisfied. Here you need to find a better way to deliver the value you create.

The following grid summarizes the different situations and responses.

Figure 3.11 The Prioritizer Grid

Satisfaction

High satisfaction low importance	High satisfaction high importance
Scrap	Cultivate
	Importance
Ignore	Develop
Low satisfaction low importance	Low satisfaction high importance

SOURCE ©CPI-Consulting

The horizontal axis depicts the value provided in relation to the importance attached to it by the customer. The vertical axis depicts the level of satisfaction derived by the customer from that value. The following two questions are asked of the customer: 'How important is X?' and 'How satisfied are you with X?'

The value offered by the company to the customer can be examined in detail. In fact, this kind of fine-tuning is the object of the exercise. The value that you offer to the customer at every point in the customer journey consists of a mix of different value elements. It is useful to identify and separate these different elements – a process known as value debundling. Each element can be given a financial value (component monetization).

Let's take a simple pot of paint as an example. Viewed from one perspective, paint is just paint. But for someone with a specific problem to solve, this perspective changes. The pot of paint quickly becomes something more than 'a product with a price'. Instead, it is now a product with different components, each of which has its own value: price, packaging, certification, colour definition, opacity, ease of use, purity level, availability, guaranteed availability in the event of repeat orders, guarantees relating to possible price variations for raw materials, etc.

For each of these components, it is possible to ask:

- 'How important is X?'
- 'How satisfied are you with X?'
- 'How much more would you be prepared to pay for X if you could be certain that X corresponds exactly to what you expect of it?'

Different customers will attach a different value to different components of your value proposition. The importance they attach to each component will reflect the environment and the conditions in which they operate.

What is valuable varies from customer to customer and moment to moment.

It is vital to remember that the things which are important for customer can change from moment to moment. When they purchase your product, 24-hour service might be low on their list of priorities. Why? Because this would have an effect on the price and at that moment the price is the most relevant aspect. But if it later transpires that your product or service has become a critical factor, then keeping it in perfect working order will suddenly have a much greater significance than previously. These are the kinds of changes in customer expectation of which you must be aware.

Consequently, your value proposition should not only be dependent on what the customer indicates is important to them at the time of initial purchase, but should also take account of a number of other possible future scenarios. You need to develop appropriate solutions and pricing strategies for each of these scenarios. For matters which are not immediately foreseen but for which a solution nonetheless exists you can justifiably charge the customer a little (or a lot) more.

But how do you identify and elaborate these alternative scenarios? By observing your customers, by talking with them and by using your imagination. By examining and understanding their business models and methods of working. By listening to what they say during their conversations with customer care. By analyzing these conversations for frequently repeated words and by restructuring the results into frequently asked questions and frequently expressed emotions.

The value components carry a different weighting from customer to customer. Some will be crucial, some not and some only partially. Once you are aware of this, it makes it possible to focus on the components that are most important to each individual customer. Other components that are less interesting can be ditched.

In this way, you can approach different customer segments in different ways, offering each of them precisely the value they most need and for which they will be willing to pay. This is called *value matching*. For instance, the basic product can be fitted with additional 'made-to-measure' value components, dependent on the segment for which it is intended. Taking the example of our pot of paint, you can focus on customers motivated by low price (basic products without extra value components), customers motivated by the need for longevity (paint that keeps its colour for several years), customers motivated by comfort (paint that is quick and easy to use), etc.

You can take this a stage further by linking particular value components to particular customer profiles or personae. This makes it possible to offer specific product-service combinations to certain categories of customer, dependent on their profiles; for example, the sale of paint in combination with an odd-jobs service. Of course, these combinations must be neatly packaged in advance as an integral product or service.

The linking of value components to customer profiles in this manner makes it possible to introduce a prompting system. This allows you to propose certain combinations of value to specific customers on the basis of their profile. A more advanced approach makes use of an online profiling questionnaire. In this case, the customer answers a series of questions in which they indicate what they want and do not want, as well as whether or not they are prepared to pay (more) for it. With this detailed information, you can make an even better made-to-measure proposal, which can form the basis for further negotiation.

If you know which value components are important and unimportant for the customer at every point of contact, and if you can map and integrate these components and the resulting cascade effect throughout the customer journey, you will be able to further develop your offer on the basis of well-informed choices. A clearly defined value proposition helps the customer to make their choice. So make sure that yours is crystal clear.

A clearly defined value proposition helps the customer to make their choice.

A customer who draws up a list of their own selection criteria and then searches the internet to find companies who can meet those criteria will find this kind of approach particularly useful. In contrast, if your value proposition is too vague or too general, you will miss the opportunity to profile your company or brand as unique or distinctive in the market.

Some companies might say 'I have an eye-catching logo' or 'my products are all orange', assuming that this is enough to ensure a distinctive identity. This is true, but only up to a point. A flashy logo and bright colours can certainly help to improve brand recognition. However, these are not factors that will persuade a customer to purchase what you are offering, unless there is an equally distinct value underlying these surface characteristics.

Customer experience design

By finding out which value components are important to the customer at every experience point during their customer journey, you can know in advance which components the customer will use to assess your performance. You can then develop your value proposition to take account of these elements, in such a way that they make a real difference for the customer, certainly in comparison with your competitors. By combining all this knowledge, you can design a complete customer experience throughout the entire length of the customer journey.

The Swedish furniture company IKEA was a pioneer in customer experience design. IKEA was the first to draw up a complete journey trajectory for its customers, from following the direction signs to its stores right through to assembling the furniture at home. It was also the first to attune its value proposition to the emotional experience of the customer. At the same time, it also continued to take full account of its own core values, which reinforced the values that made the customers so enthusiastic.

The entire customer journey was visualized with a methodology developed by G-CEM, a company that develops models to optimize customer experience management.

The different contact points are mapped in a linear process in time. The final contact point is most important, since this determines the feeling with which the customer leaves the store. IKEA allows its customers to experience how the positive value of a visit to their store (low price, modern design, etc) far exceeds the negative effort involved (busy car parks, long waits at the check-out, do-it-yourself assembly, etc).

IKEA is a budget-friendly furniture and lifestyle store. Budget-friendly means that it tries to keep costs as low as possible. This is something that the company makes visible. You have to collect your furniture yourself from huge shelved areas. The furniture is packed in simple cardboard boxes. Some parts of the stores are sparsely decorated. There are few staff, so that customers sometimes have to wait before they can ask questions.

But these negatives are more than balanced by the positives: trendy design furniture at cheap prices, other cheap and unexpected fun articles, exotic meals at rock-bottom prices in the restaurant, etc. IKEA deliberately does little to reduce the long queues at the check-out, but makes up for this with a stand for hot-dogs, ice-cream and soft drinks next to the exit, again at give-away prices. This sends people home with a smile.[19]

For customers, the IKEA story rings true. IKEA does not stand for quick; it stands for budget-friendly – and that is what it delivers. If it ever tries to jazz up its stores by raising its prices or dropping the quality in its restaurant, it would no longer be the authentic blue-yellow IKEA that so many of us know and love. Its customer experience would change dramatically and its concept would fail.

Why over-delivery is not good

'Under-promise and over-deliver' is a popular phrase in Anglo-Saxon sales circles. It means that you should try and do more than you promise. This is actually what many companies attempt. They assume that this will result in the customer praising them to the heavens. Many sales staff now feel obliged to behave in this manner, almost to the extent that it has become routine, with the salesperson as a kind of master-fixer. But is it really as beneficial as everyone thinks?

One of the problems with over-delivery is that often there are no internal agreements within the company about what it means. And even if there are, sales staff quickly deviate from them because that one particular customer is so important, isn't she? And we all want to make our targets for the quarter, don't we? One seller offers 10 extra samples. Another gives an additional 3 per cent discount. A third throws in an extra 20 kilos. Soon everyone is at it.

A second problem is that this exaggerated commercial zeal soon comes to be regarded as standard practice, even by the customer, a situation which the smart ones know how to exploit. Some years ago, I was involved in a review of the commercial strategy of an industrial textile company. The atmosphere in the sales team was not good and I was asked to find out why. It soon became clear that all the sales staff were demotivated.

But the reason why only became apparent when I spoke to the CEO. It was not so much what he said to me. It was the way his phone was constantly ringing throughout our interview. Each time, he stopped our discussion to answer it. The calls were all from customers who had a hot-line direct to the boss! And they all asked the same thing: could he perhaps do 'a little more' for their forthcoming order? They all knew that the option existed to bypass the sales team and go straight to the top.

And the top man then phoned down to his sales staff to tell them that he had already done the deal with their customers. No wonder they lacked motivation! Perhaps the CEO got a kick out of this sort of thing; who can say? What is certain is that the company – and the sales team – performed much better after the CEO had been replaced.

Recent research in the US has further undermined the myth of 'under-promise and over-deliver'[20]. Behavioural scientists Ayelet Gneezy of the University of California in San Diego and Nicholas Epley of the University of Chicago investigated whether or not doing more than you promised actually results in a lasting effect on those who benefit from it.

The researchers developed a series of tests that examined the reactions of test subjects who received more than they expected, less than they expected or precisely what they expected. In one test, for example, the participants were asked to remember how they had reacted in the past when a promise was matched exactly, or less or more than expected. In another experiment, they were asked to solve a series of puzzles, assisted by a helper.

There were three groups of helpers. The first group didn't help at all. The second group helped just enough. The third group did everything they could to help. After the puzzles were completed, the impact of the helper was measured.

All these tests showed that attempts to impress someone (a test subject, a customer, etc) by doing more than you promised are simply wasted effort. It does not result in a greater feeling of gratitude or appreciation in the beneficiary of your generosity.

A surprising result? Perhaps. It certainly surprised Gneezy and Epley, who had expected to discover a moderately positive effect. Nicholas Epley compared a promise lodged in our mind with a kind of contract, which automatically governs our further expectations. If somebody promises us something, we expect them as a minimum to do what they have promised. But we also have a general tendency to expect that they will do a little bit more – because we regard doing any less as unfair and therefore morally unacceptable.

This explains why it is crucial for your reputation to always do what you promise. It also explains why doing more is unnecessary: people half expect it anyway and consequently are not grateful when it happens.

Invest in keeping your promises, but not exceeding them.

There is, however, one exception: being competitive in terms of price, by offering a little more than was first agreed, is not the same as trying to create additional unrequested value, with which you seek to enthuse the customer. Invest your time and effort in a strong value proposition – and then stick to it. Do no more, but also no less.

It is always better to do what you initially promised, rather than trying to make things up as you go along. You can certainly promise more than your rivals are promising: this is straightforward competition. After all, your objective is to make your customer go 'wow'. Make your offer to the customer as clear as you can. If you can't do it with words alone, do it through images and through your own behaviour. Make sure that your communication is unambiguous and consistent. And don't forget to check that everyone in the company is on the same wavelength.

Notes

1   Kotler, P, Saunders, J, Wong, V, Broere, F, & Armstrong, G (2009) *Principes van Marketing*, 5th edn, Pearson Benelux bv, Amsterdam
2   Kraljic, P (1983) Purchasing must become supply management, *Harvard Business Review*, Sept, pp109–17
3   The classic sales process based on the funnel approach takes little or no account of the after-sales period and the possible development of customer loyalty. It is equally impervious to the iterations made by customers during the sales process, which may prompt them to investigate the offers of competing suppliers or to unexpectedly add or remove new specifications from their initial set of requirements and expectations.

4   Court, D, Elzinga, D, Mulder, S and Vetvik, O J [accessed May 2015] The
     consumer decision journey, *McKinsey & Company* [Online] http://
     www.mckinsey.com/insights/marketing_sales/the_consumer_decision_
     journey

5   Maes, Patrick (2013) *Sales 3.0*, CPI-Consulting

6   Woollaston, Victoria [accessed May 2017] EasyJet launches 'Sneakairs': Smart
     shoes fitted with sensors VIBRATE to help direct wearers around new cities,
     Daily Mail [Online] http://www.dailymail.co.uk/sciencetech/article-3588413/
     EasyJet-launches-Sneakairs-Smart-shoes-fitted-sensors-VIBRATE-help-direct-
     wearers-new-cities.html

7   Robarts, Stu [accessed May 2017] easyJet smart shoes let you follow your
     feet, *New Atlas* [Online] http://newatlas.com/easyjet-barcelona-street-
     project-sneakairs/43369/

8   Wikipedia [accessed July 2015] Persona (user experience) [Online] https://
     en.wikipedia.org/wiki/Persona_(user_experience)

9   Court, D *et al* [accessed May 2015]

10   SALESManago [accessed Dec 2017] Marketing Automation – The Definitive
     and Ultimate Guide to Marketing Automation [Online] https://
     www.salesmanago.com/info/definitve_and_ultimate_new_knowledge.htm

11   Microsoft Canada [accessed May 2015] Attention Spans – Consumer Insights,
     Microsoft.com [Online] http://advertising.microsoft.com/en/cl/31966/
     how-does-digital-affect-canadian-attention-spans

12   Statistic Brain Research Institute [accessed May 2017] 15 statistics that should
     change the business world – but haven't, Statistic Brain [Online] http://
     www.statisticbrain.com/attention-span-statistics/

13   Moth, D [accessed August 2015] Site speed: case studies, tips and tools for
     improving your conversion rate, *econsultancy* [Online] https://econsultancy.
     com/blog/10936-site-speed-case-studies-tips-and-tools-for-improving-your-
     conversion-rate/

14   Statistic Brain Research Institute [accessed May 2017]

15   Northridge Group [accessed August 2015] The State of Customer
     Service Experience 2015 [Online] http://www.northridgegroup.com/
     The-State-of-Customer-Service-Experience

16   Shankman, P [accessed August 2015] The greatest customer service story ever
     told, starring Morton's steakhouse, *Shankman.com* [Online] http://shankman.com/
     the-best-customer-service-story-ever-told-starring-mortons-steakhouse/

17   Konrad, Alex [accessed May 2015] Salesforce Innovation Secrets: How Marc
     Benioff's Team Stays On Top, *Forbes* [Online] http://www.forbes.com/sites/
     alexkonrad/2014/08/20/marc-benioffs-innovation-secret/

18   Pulizzi, J [accessed September 2015] How Content Marketing
     Can Save the Book Industry, *Content Marketing Institute*

[Online] http://contentmarketinginstitute.com/2012/09/
how-content-marketing-can-save-the-book-industry/

19 Harzevoort, S [accessed May 2015] Drie Nederlandse topmerken over
customer experience management, *Marketing Tribune* [Online] http://
www.marketingtribune.nl/b2b/nieuws/2013/11/drie-nederlandse-topmerken-
over-customer-experience-management31_0/index. xml

20 Stillman, Jessica [accessed April 2015] Why 'Underpromise and Overdeliver'
is Terrible Advice, *Inc.com* [Online] http://www.inc.com/jessica-stillman/
underpromise-and-overdeliver-is-terrible-advice.html

PART THREE
Turning opportunity into sales results

Using people and resources within your disruption strategy

Disruptive selling has an impact on every phase of the sales process. Consequently, it is a good idea to look at each phase separately and to reassign the roles and responsibilities of your sales organization. Focus on the distribution of tasks and the collaboration between sales, marketing and customer service.

Most companies still expect sales people to run after every lead.

The times they are a-changin'

During the 1960s and 1970s, sales teams were trained in accordance with the principles of Gitomer and Ogilvy. For many sales staff, books like *The Little Red Book of Selling* were constantly on their bedside tables, trustworthy bibles that offered them comfort during sleepless nights. These principles have not all been jettisoned in subsequent years. The basics of Gitomer's 'sales greatness' and the importance of having clear propositions for specific target groups, as argued by Ogilvy, are still the cornerstones of a successful sales approach.

Add to this models for account management and solution selling, and you have the perfect package of tools that every seller, marketeer or supply chain officer needs to master.

All these principles serve the same purpose: they tell the seller how to approach prospects, how to turn leads into contracts, and how to maintain a good customer relationship once the sale has been made.

The period from the 1960s until well into the 1980s (and in some cases the 1990s) was the period when the division between marketing and sales was absolute. Marketing provided the brochures and printed matter that filled the briefcases of the sales reps, who handed them out to their prospects: 'Would you like to know more? You will find everything you need in this nice brochure, complete with informative texts, glossy photos and full technical specifications.'

From the 1990s onwards this printed material was supplemented with a website, and contact was now made not only by phone but also by email. The salespeople circled above the entire process like eagles. They were the lead contacts who saw everything, knew everything and communicated exclusively with the customers. They were also responsible for steering and following up the activities of the internal service, the order service, the supply chain and the fulfilment.

Each day they went on their travels, the boots of their cars stuffed with brochures, presentation material, demo products and samples. A series of prospects and customers were visited, following which an entry was made into the customer database. And 12 months later, the same salesperson went to visit the same customers all over again. We might reasonably call this the traditional approach to modern sales: *Sales 1.0*.[1]

For salespeople, this was a time of great freedom. But as we all know... times change. The sales process became more complex and was followed more closely, both by companies and customers. Savings needed to be made. New thinking and innovation were required. 'Efficiency' and 'effectiveness' popped up as the new buzzwords. It was no longer acceptable for all the information about customers to be stored in the heads of the sales eagles.

A reorganization of tasks was urgently needed and as time passed this gradually became easier. The first CRM systems were introduced. From then on, the relationship with the customer needed to be managed. All suspects, prospects, addresses, negotiates, closings and orders were henceforth kept systematically. What's more, this systemization made it easier to monitor and steer sales, since it meant that the sales team knew at any given moment which customers were hot. The subsequent arrival of portable computers, remote connections and tablets made it possible to better prepare visits, access real-time information and even update your presentation at the very last minute.

In the world of sales and marketing, the introduction of these new possibilities had the effect of a small earthquake. It meant sales evolved from black box selling (with sales controlling all the information about prospects and customers) to a model where information was shared throughout the organization. We might reasonably call this new approach *Sales 2.0*.[2]

Sales 2. 0 ensured that the role of the internal service became more important in most companies. Customers found it beneficial to have someone they could phone, who gave answers to questions quickly and accurately, had access to data about orders and customer histories, and was also in direct contact with the planners, maintenance teams and technicians. The application of the Sales 2. 0 model immediately resulted in an explosion of usable customer and prospect data. Segmentation and targeting were easier than ever before, as was the measuring of the impact of marketing actions against concrete results.

But this was not the most far-reaching change because Sales 2. 0 focused on leads as the start of sales cycle, the task of generating leads switched increasingly to marketing. The sales staff were now responsible for converting these leads into customers. One consequence of this development was a dramatic decrease in the importance and share of 'cold calling' in sales work.

The moment was now ripe for the emergence of *Sales 3.0*.[3] The company website grew in importance and was equipped with all the very latest communication tools. The performance of the technology improved rapidly and was used increasingly to structure the sales process. The customer also began to venture more and more online and, in particular, on social media.

These media quickly became both a source of information for feeding the CRM and a possible source of both good and bad publicity. Conversation managers were appointed to monitor and steer these new phenomena and soon every self-respecting company was on Facebook and LinkedIn.

Connecting with the customer was now the priority and the need to do this in real time swiftly became imperative. This required the development of bigger and better CRM systems, so that the mass of data could be processed, contacts better prepared, customer needs more precisely analysed, and the outcomes more closely followed up. The work terrain of sales switched more and more away from visits and more and more towards Skype, the telephone and social media.

The previous three paragraphs were deliberately written in the past tense, because disruptive selling goes far beyond Sales 3.0. Today, it is customers who take the lead – but they expect to be guided and accompanied throughout every stage of the customer decision journey. And it is a long journey: from the moment they first consider a purchase to the moment they consider making a new one.

In disruptive selling it is the task of everyone in the company to take good care of the customer relationship. There must be no artificial walls between sales, marketing and customer service. They must be integrated into a single sales process. Their respective responsibilities must overlap and merge into each other because the value experience of the customer is central, and it must be safeguarded by every employee in every section of the organization.

In this way, for example, product and portfolio management and the manner in which valued is offered to the customer are also an integral part of the integrated sales process. The common goal is to optimize the company's chosen customer experience, in the expectation that this will persuade people to buy your products and services.

> Stop selling, start helping.
> The new sales model results in a crisis of identity for many traditional sales people. They will need to retrain or disappear.

The purpose of the new sales organization is no longer to sell something – anything – to the customer. The modern salesperson now seeks to help the customer, to provide them with the specific value they want, in accordance with their needs and wishes. This radical role reversal will not come about simply by creating new functions and new departments. It will also be necessary to invest in new processes, new technology and – above all – people.

In most cases, a revision of the commercial approach will also be necessary, resulting in a redistribution and a reinvention of the company's talent. Some new people with new skills will need to be attracted. Others, who are unable to adjust to the new situation or whose function has become redundant in the new business model, will need to be let go.

What's more, this change is not just a one-off: it is an ongoing process. You must be prepared to regularly reassess your structure and your approach, making adjustments as and where necessary. This will not be possible with procedures that take weeks to update or with annual brainstormings around the Kaizen approach, lean management and permanent improvement.

If you want to introduce disruptive selling with success, there are three core values that you need to make central – and they all begin with the letter 'A'.

The Triple-A model: authenticity, accountability and agility

Authenticity, accountability and agility are the three core values that will ensure that the customer experience is maximized throughout the customer journey. It was with this in mind that CPI developed the Triple-A model.

Table 4.1 Sales 3.0: a functional model

SALES 3.0			
MARKETING	**SALES**	**SALES**	**CUSTOMER SERVICE**
• Marketing takes responsibility for managing the customer journey before, during and after the sale. • Marketing generates qualified leads	• Sales ensures that qualified prospects become customers. • Sales visits become an exception.	• Sales works via the telephone, email, social media and video chats	• Customer service is the hub of relational management. • Customers are assisted proactively. • Upselling and cross-selling are tasks for customer service.
DIGITAL AND SOCIAL RELEVANCE			
Presence on social media and the internet is the basis of every sales strategy.		Relevant content, easy accessibility via all types of devices, a quick response to questions and a position as a trusted advisor are essential.	
INNOVATION			
Innovation relates to products and services. Innovation is created in collaboration with customers.		The innovation process is based on smart partnerships. Business model disruption is an objective in itself.	
TECHNOLOGY			
Technology is an enabler. Marketing automation and business intelligence make the defference in customer engagement and marketing power		Smart collaborative tools replace email and reduce meetings.	
MANAGEMENT AND CONTROL			
Management is carried out on the basis of objectives and the periodic monitoring of key results.		Inspiring, enthusing, enabling and empowering staff in the most important role of managers and team leaders.	

SOURCE ©CPI-Consulting

Figure 4.1 The Triple-A model

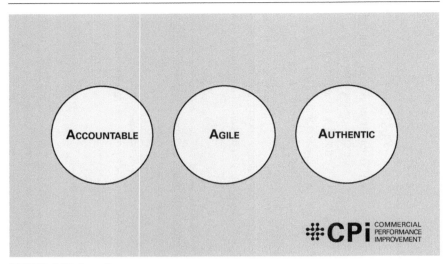

SOURCE ©CPI-Consulting

Authenticity

Authenticity is about always being there for your customers. It means that they continually feel that you are taking good care of them. This is only possible because you know at every moment what your customer really wants. You understand their behaviour and their preferences. The information that you have gathered via your marketing technology makes it possible to analyse their needs and take appropriate action.

The more interactions you have with the customer and the more data your CRM system collects, the easier this will become. Your image of the customer will come into sharper focus, so that you can make your offer increasingly personal and made-to-measure – for example, with content that refers to the customer's individual context.

By linking the individual customer profile to the personae in your CRM, you will be able to recognize and even predict potential problems. This will allow you to solve them almost before they arise by proposing tried-and-tested solutions. After a number of personalized interventions of this kind, the customer will start to feel comfortable in the relationship.

And because the customer profile is automatically enriched with new data and reworked, your staff will have to spend less time trying to investigate and interpret what customers really want. This will leave them with more space to provide meaningful help. At the same time, this also relieves the pressure on your own people, so that they feel more relaxed and perform better.

Accountability

Accountability is necessary to give your staff the opportunity to develop their own potential, by showing what they can do. It also guarantees the value of their performance for both the company and the customer. You must measure what it costs to use people and resources in certain circumstances and balance this against the current and future profit that you can expect to generate from each prospect or customer.

This costing exercise is based on two underlying principles. The first is 'cost to sell', which relates to the full trajectory of lead generation until the moment of purchase; in other words, how much it costs to sell someone something. The second is 'cost to serve': how much does it cost to provide the customer with the information and services that are necessary to persuade them to remain a customer.

Naturally, both concepts are further linked to marketing expenditure and the costs that are incurred to keep the whole sales and marketing structure operational. It is particularly important when making decisions about the use of technology that you have a clear understanding of the full cost of the sales cycle.

Accountability is more necessary today than it was in the past. Why? Because you will need to make a number of investments in marketing automation and afterwards will want to know what return these investments yield in combination with your staff and your campaigns. In my experience relatively few companies have a good understanding of their 'cost to sell' and 'cost to serve'. Many of these costs remain hidden. For example, with the older systems it is not easy to accurately assess the true cost of a salesperson who is out on the road each day.

Contact or touchpoint tracking does now make this possible, on the basis of concrete data that can be allocated to an individual member of staff or a team. This allows you to make decisions based on hard facts and figures, resulting in a much more efficient sales organization, in which the ROI of investments can be maximized.

Accountability also helps to make people responsible for reaching set targets and results. Today's employees generally want more freedom and responsibility. The era of 'command and control' is long gone. It has been replaced by staff who are no longer judged simply on the basis of their attendance, but on the basis of their results. The way they generate these results is now at their own discretion. Managing on the basis of results means that it is necessary to measure and assess these results, offsetting the costs that were incurred to achieve them.

Wildcards for customer care

Before I started CPI, I worked for a number of years as an organizational adviser. Whenever we visited a company, our objective was always to do more with less. This led to the introduction of strict rules and criteria that only reflected the interests of the company. In essence, the aim was to maximize return on every single minute worked. This sounds good on paper and looks even better in spreadsheets.

Once during an audit, when I was observing the activities of a customer service centre, a telephone call was received from a small customer. She had a problem with a delivery and was clearly not well organized. The conversation dragged on and on, sometimes drifting off into personal issues. The boss of the company was in hospital and his wife was doing her best to keep the ship afloat in his absence. Even so, the bills were piling up and now this crucial order had gone wrong as a result of a silly mistake.

The operator deliberately turned his back on me and tried to find a solution for his increasingly desperate woman caller. The conversation ultimately lasted about 20 minutes. But at the end even this small customer had the feeling that the company cared about her. And the operator had the feeling that his intervention had made a difference. After he had hung up, he turned to me and said: 'If you want to get me sacked for spending so much time on that call, I can't stop you. But if I hadn't done it, I couldn't have looked at myself in the mirror. And we'd have lost a customer.'

Naturally, I 'forgot' to include this case in my final report, but I never forgot the incident and it prompted me to look for a more positive approach to my professional life. In particular, it inspired me to develop the concept of the Customer Service Wildcard.

I now advise my customers to give their own customer service workers a number of 'free' minutes per call hour. During these minutes they can do things their own way, without the need to take account of the normal rules of cost to serve and cost to sell. By carefully quantifying this 'free' time, it is possible to keep the total 'cost to serve' within reasonable and agreed limits, while allowing the operators to adopt a more human approach.

Wildcards are a guarantee for authenticity and ensure that your people can make a difference when it really counts.

Agility

The need for agility refers to both the attitude of staff and the attitude or culture of the organization as a whole. Companies are increasingly confronted with developments over which they no longer have control. Customer expectation is one good example. A competitor entering the market with a disruptive business model is another. Technology is also constantly improving all the time.

Change can, of course, be beneficial. It is therefore important that a company is able to respond to change with speed and flexibility. This is what we mean by agility. Agility requires an organizational model in which people can adjust and be redeployed quickly. And the technology stack must be organized in such a way that components can be switched or replaced without disruption.

Nowadays, software tools evolve at high speed. This means that monitoring new products and assessing whether or not they can be added beneficially to your system has become an almost daily task. Tools are replaced more quickly than ever before. At least, they are if you want to keep up in the competitive race. As a result, software is seldom bought these days; instead, it is leased on a subscription basis. You won't change your CRM system every six months, but you probably will change the tracker that screens the online behaviour of your customers.

Many companies still feel the need for a degree of permanence, to arrange things for a longer period of time. This is a mistake. In the new sales era the situation is constantly fluid. It is important to continuously question whether your company is 'fit for purpose', in terms of its approach, talent and IT tools.

In particular, your tools require close monitoring, because new ones are appearing all the time. In the old days, replacing a tool after six months was seen as a sign of failure. Today, you should be worrying if you are not considering a new alternative every four months! It is crucial to keep your eye on the technological ball, constantly evaluating new innovations, weighing them up against your current system, replacing elements if necessary, and then starting the same evaluation/replacement exercise all over again.

Agility means that you set clear objectives, linked to key results and a lean strategy to achieve those results. This implies the need to test things, assess things and replace things, repeating the process on a regular basis. This keeps your company sharp and focused.

The evaluation cycle that I apply in CPI to monitor our objectives and key results (OKR) runs over a period of 12 weeks. This is also what we recommend to our customers. This means that you examine everything you do at least once every three months. Sometimes we even shorten the evaluation period to six weeks.

Consider, for example, a sales objective. The sales results for six weeks are probably linked to a sales process, traffic building, lead generation, etc. In other words, they are linked to an organizational structure, processes and technology. For the first six weeks, sales are made in accordance with the agreed procedures and the available tools. At the end of that six weeks, the results are noted. During the following six weeks, the same procedures and tools are kept. However, investigations are made to see where adjustments, new technology or organizational change are necessary.

The aim is then to test these conclusions in the subsequent six-week period. This results in a cycle of 18 weeks in total. In other words, after 18 weeks you have identified and implemented the necessary changes to improve your sales process.

Authenticity, agility and accountability form part of a culture. Every culture is made or broken by people. Consequently, your staff need to adjust to the culture – or be made to fit. But the factor that most facilitates a Triple-A culture is marketing technology. This provides you with crucial and constantly updated insights about your customers and their position in the sales process.

Marketing technology helps you to understand your prospects and customers better. And if you understand them better, you can serve them better in the moment, allowing you to develop a more correct and a more sustainable relationship.

In the past, some people were also made accountable for their results. But this was often a hit-and-miss affair. Nowadays, however, marketing technology makes it possible to measure customer behaviour and evaluate/allocate the effects of marketing efforts and sales actions in a much more objective manner. The same is true of agility. Thanks to the sheer variety of new tools, companies can now respond quicker and more efficiently to changes in consumer behaviour.

But this can only be realized within a framework of concrete objectives, in which the key results of every employee are defined and systematically monitored. People must then be given the necessary resources and responsibility to achieve these objectives. It is worth repeating: the days of 'command and control' are long gone. The most important task of today's managers and team leaders is to inspire, enthuse, enable and empower their colleagues.

Working with objectives and key results

Since the 1950s, companies have introduced numerous techniques in an effort to improve the performance of their staff. Peter Drucker introduced management by objectives (MBO). During the 1980s, SMART objectives and key performance indicators (KPIs) became popular.

OKR stands for 'objectives and key results'. The concept was first introduced at Google in 1999 by venture capitalist John Doerr. It enabled the company to grow from an organization of just 40 employees to a worldwide mastodon with 40,000 staff, which has changed the way we live and work.

Figure 4.2　The OKR model

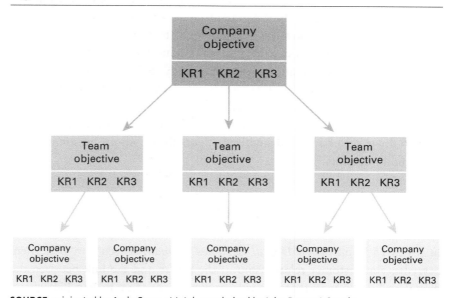

SOURCE originated by Andy Grove at Intel, popularized by John Doerr at Google

If you want your company and your people to be agile, it is useful to work with key objectives and results. The application of OKR helps to enhance the ambition level of both the organization and the individual employees, and allows their respective objectives to be closely aligned.

It is worth the effort to define time-limited and measurable objectives and key results for every level and every function. These objectives and key results must be shared transparently throughout the company. In this way, people will feel more personally involved with the objectives of the company as a whole, by underlining the importance of their personal contribution to the higher goal.

If you want to make a start with OKR, you can make use of fun software like Weekdone, in which your staff can fill in a satisfaction score. This is a good way to deal with the necessary end-of-week reporting, incorporating the elements that we always recommend to our CPI customers: progress – plans – problems. Each employee can add a few lines of comments about each of these themes, explaining what has happened during the past week and outlining the plan for the next one.

An objective must be formulated for every member of staff, linked to a maximum of five key results. The objective must be ambitious but also achievable for both the company and the employee concerned. The key results must be time-limited, measurable and must make the achievement of the objective possible if the results are met.

For example, 'land a man on Mars by 2025' is an objective. For the organization concerned – NASA, for instance – the key results might be: 'Develop and test a rocket for a return flight to Mars by 2020'; 'Build a space accommodation module that weighs no more than 500 kg by 2022'; 'Select and train astronauts for the mission by 2024'. In turn, these key results become objectives for lower levels in the organization, each requiring their own set of key objectives to achieve success.

In this way, the ambitious objective of the organization as a whole is broken down into a series of smaller but equally ambitious personal objectives and key results.

Digital becomes human

In his 2015 book *When Digital Becomes Human*, Steven Van Belleghem describes the customer relationship of the future and the link between the digital and the human that this will involve.[4] According to Van Belleghem, most companies recognize that they have ground to make up in technological terms, but overestimate the quality of the contact between their human staff and their customers. 'Just because your company currently works with people, this does not mean that these people bring sufficient added value to the relationship.'

Van Belleghem predicts that companies without a digital backbone will not survive. 'As a result of strong digitalization, the human contact between customer and company will continue to fall each year. But something that becomes scarce inevitably increases in value. This is an old and immutable economic law. It means that the less personal contact there is in a customer relationship, the more important it becomes. This analysis therefore requires a double transformation for every organization: a digital one and a human one.'

Both dimensions can create value for the customer. Consequently, it is wise to give full consideration to them both in strategic terms: 'A company is best advised to make use of the predictive power of data and the creative chaos of human talent. Every forward-thinking organization should consider the introduction of self-service systems for its customers, backed up by a system of human support.'

How can this combination of the digital and the human be translated into an effective sales approach? Where do you focus on automated processes? When will you use your scarce and valuable human resources? What can you do to build up customer loyalty, so that relationships become sustainable in the long term? These and a thousand and one other questions will require a full analysis of all the functions, roles, responsibilities and structures in your organization.

The rise of the marketeer

The Economist Intelligence Unit Ltd published an interesting report in 2015, about future changes in the marketing world: *The Rise of the Marketeer: Driving engagement, experience and revenue.*[5] The report was the result of a survey conducted amongst 478 chief marketing officers and senior marketing executives worldwide. A third of the respondents work in Europe.

What follows are its findings.

Change agent

The large majority of the marketeers thought that the time has now come to give the marketing function a new dimension. More than four in five want a different structure and design for marketing organization. In Europe, more than 90 per cent hold this opinion, in comparison with 72 per cent in the US – which suggests that the old continent has some catching up to do.

If the figures are viewed from the opposite end, just 19 per cent of marketeers think that no change is necessary; in five years' time, they expect to be working in the same manner as today, while 52 per cent feel that some change is inevitable, but would prefer to see it happen step by step. For them, change is an incremental progression, a gradual evolution.

Only 29 per cent are in favour of radical and immediate change. 'These are the change agents,' says the report. 'In comparison with their more conservative colleagues, these "corporate revolutionaries" are more likely to be seen as a cost centre, and they aspire to drive revenue, to be accountable for managing the end-to-end customer experience and engagement, to move aggressively to acquire talent and to actively leverage data and technology.'

Customer experience

The study also showed that marketing is increasingly becoming the driving force behind the provision of optimum customer experience. Everyone in the company has contact with the customer at some point. Marketeers want to make more use of marketing automation to keep an overview of all these contacts and to manage the customer experience from beginning to end. This in turn predicts fewer touchpoints with sales and customer support teams, and a slight increase with product management and finance.

Hunting for new skills

The gap between what marketeers were used to doing in the past and what they will need to do in the future has never been wider. Four out of every ten respondents want to surround themselves with talent and expertise in the fields of digital engagement and marketing technology.

More than half expect that the internet of things will revolutionize the marketing discipline by 2020. Widespread accessibility to real-time, personalized and mobile communication is seen as another factor likely to have a major impact.

New investments

Three-quarters of the most frequently cited planned investments are focused on omni-channel communication with the customer: social networks, mobile applications and email. The fourth most popular investment is data analysis (in particular, dealing with big data). There is a general desire to amalgamate coordinated and uncoordinated data from different sources, in order to paint a sharper picture of the customer and their needs, wants and intentions.

Marketing as a source of income

Management guru Peter Drucker once said that the task of marketing was to make sales unnecessary. By and large, marketing is still generally seen as a cost centre. But within three to five years, four out of every five companies will see marketing as a revenue driver. Marketing will be given new responsibilities and will be judged on the extent to which it is able to meet those responsibilities successfully. From now on, income generation is the name of the game.

Marketing will be increasingly seen as a revenue driver.

Changes in sales, marketing and customer service

It is difficult to predict how the functions of sales, marketing and customer support will evolve during the next five years. It will still always be necessary to make a sale – that will never change – but the sale process now involves so much more, both before and after the moment of purchase. In this respect, a number of clear trends are discernible.

The first is, of course, the need to take *a broader view of the sales experience*. We have already discussed this at length. The ability to offer a positive experience to the customer at all touchpoints and through all available channels in all the different phases of the customer journey, from the moment of first contact with your products until the moment they (hopefully) become an ambassador, is the key to success in the modern marketplace.

A second important trend is a growing awareness of the need for *social and digital relevance*. Being present on the internet and in social media is the foundation of your sales strategy. Developing relevant content is nowadays essential. But this content must be capable of being accessed easily through all channels and on every different kind of smartphone, tablet and wearable (smart watches, intelligent clothing, etc).

It is equally important to have a high-degree of open-mindedness to suggestions from the market and a willingness to respond to questions quickly and expertly. This means that you need to manage these media in three different dimensions: the provision of relevant content, the expansion of your reach and the maintenance of your structural relations with the prospect and the customer. Your objective is to become a trusted adviser. But you need to keep your advice entertaining as well as informative.

Remember that the attention span of your customers is shrinking all the time, and the communication pressure from your competitors is on the increase.

The third key trend is *innovation*. Innovation ensures that you remain interesting for your customers. This innovation relates not only to your

Figure 4.3 The Sales 3.0 stage model

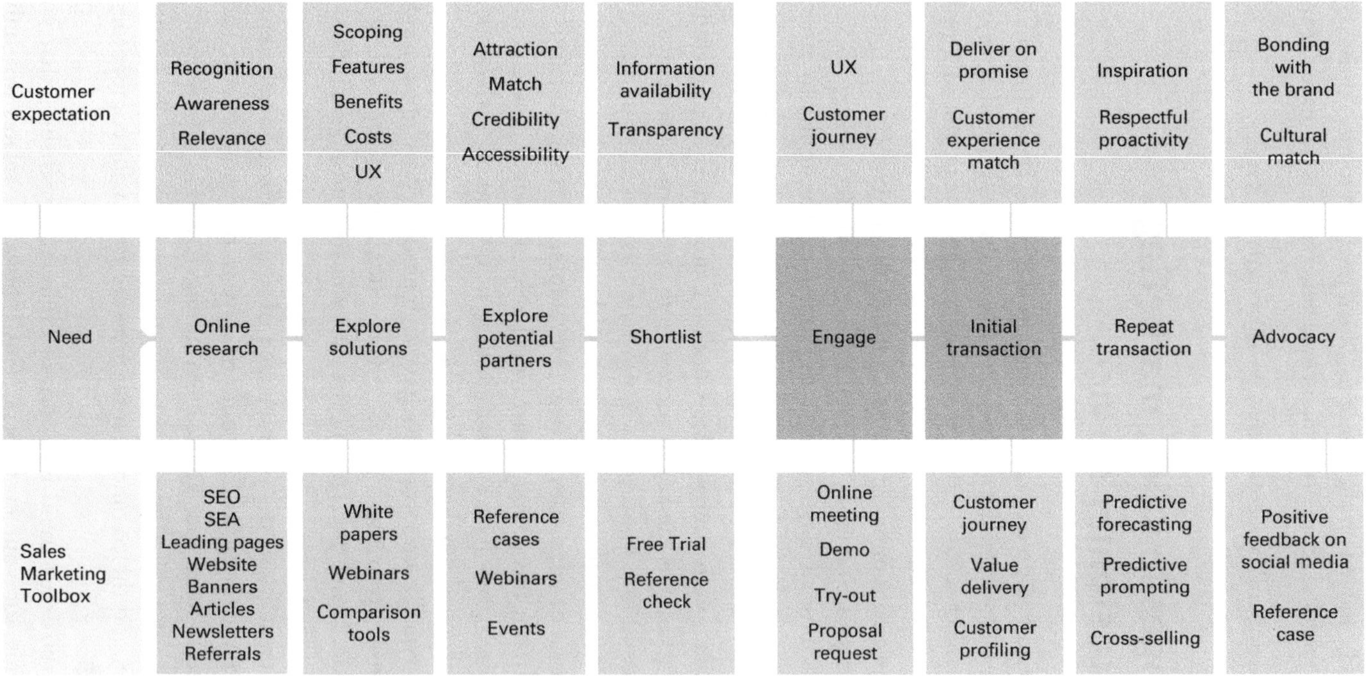

Customer expectation	Recognition / Awareness / Relevance	Scoping / Features / Benefits / Costs / UX	Attraction / Match / Credibility / Accessibility	Information availability / Transparency	UX / Customer journey	Deliver on promise / Customer experience match	Inspiration / Respectful proactivity	Bonding with the brand / Cultural match
Need	Online research	Explore solutions	Explore potential partners	Shortlist	Engage	Initial transaction	Repeat transaction	Advocacy
Sales Marketing Toolbox	SEO / SEA / Leading pages / Website / Banners / Articles / Newsletters / Referrals	White papers / Webinars / Comparison tools	Reference cases / Webinars / Events	Free Trial / Reference check	Online meeting / Demo / Try-out / Proposal request	Customer journey / Value delivery / Customer profiling	Predictive forecasting / Predictive prompting / Cross-selling	Positive feedback on social media / Reference case

SOURCE ©CPI-Consulting

products and services, but also to your business model. This means you need to look at the way people can pay, the way you help them after the sale, the way you collaborate with other partners to provide a trouble-free customer experience, etc.

The fourth trend is the *growing impact of technology*. In general, the organization of the sales function is becoming more technological. Marketing automation, CRM and business intelligence can all make the difference in terms of customer engagement and marketing power. The analysis of data, the correct reading and interpretation of metrics, the ability to recognize data patterns, the capacity to react flexibly via the right channel with the right message, the targeted adjustment of marketing and sales actions: these and various other technological functions mean that marketing, sales and customer service are fast becoming analytical sciences. The aim is to provide accurate insights at the ideal moment, fed by a continuous data stream produced by the customer and, increasingly, by the internet of things.

As a result of these developments, existing software, tools and devices that are used to manage customer data, customer profiles, project management and process management will need to be integrated into a more coherent system. This will require more powerful technology to run it.

But how exactly do these trends affect the functions of marketing, sales and customer service in practical terms?

Marketeers will continue to work on websites and brand awareness. Flyers and brochures will still be needed. Seminars and congresses will still be organized. True, the flyers will probably no longer be printed and the seminars will be virtual rather than physical. But the basic principles of *awareness creation* and *brand building* will remain. However, marketing will also be given the responsibility for co-managing the sales cycle and lead generation, before, during and after the customer's purchase. If a customer buys once, you want them to buy again – and for this you need marketing.

As a result, marketeers will be given data that makes it possible for them to put together a made-to-measure value package for each individual prospect and customer. This means that they will need to analyse customer needs more deeply, create segments, seek targets, define customer profiles and target groups, and develop innovative and creative value propositions for each of them.

The objective is to provide the prospect or customer with a series of experiences that encourages them to move voluntarily through the sales funnel in the direction of a (new) purchase. New marketeers will be expected to have good knowledge of the customer journeys for the different customer profiles. They must be able to analyse and interpret data; be familiar with marketing technology; be creative enough to offer the prospect or customer precisely the value and the experience they expect at every different phase of the purchase journey.

This requires a degree of commercial feeling. If someone asks you for product information, you don't ask in return for their VAT number. If someone has downloaded a paper from your website and spent time reading your articles, you don't need to be a genius to appreciate that they might value an invitation to a webinar.

Managing customer experience is totally different from bringing a product to market. Exit the marketing manager? Yes and no. In the near future the function will be known as 'experience manager'. Or perhaps that role exists already. The abbreviation of Customer Experience Officer is also CEO – and not without good reason!

> There is no value in having more leads if they offer no prospect of a later sale.
> Bad leads only cost money.

The intrinsic quality of leads is becoming ever-more important. This was made clear in the *2015 Demand Gen Report Benchmark Study*. Three quarters of the top marketeers who were questioned said that in future they wish to concentrate on lead quality rather than quantity. This is only logical. There is no value in having more leads if they offer no prospect of a later sale. Bad leads only cost money.

In the years ahead, it is marketing that will need to provide these high-quality leads. In particular, marketing automation will make it possible to assess the real potential of individual leads, allowing the wheat to be separated from the chaff. It will also be possible to determine in which phase of the sales funnel each marketing-qualified lead is situated at any given moment. This will make it easier to determine what further action is necessary to move the lead on to the next phase. In this way, marketing will be given the responsibility for converting marketing-qualified leads into sales-qualified leads (SQLs).

The moment when the lead can be categorized as 'sales-ready' is dependent on criteria that you can select and set in your CRM. For example, is there a strong likelihood that the lead will be persuaded to make a first purchase by sales within a fixed period of time? However, the basis for these criteria must always be a comparison of possible expenditure against possible income.

In general, you will be able to see when someone is ready to make a purchase from the kinds of questions they ask, the papers they download from your website and their other online activity.

Figure 4.4   From TOFU through MOFU to BOFU[6]

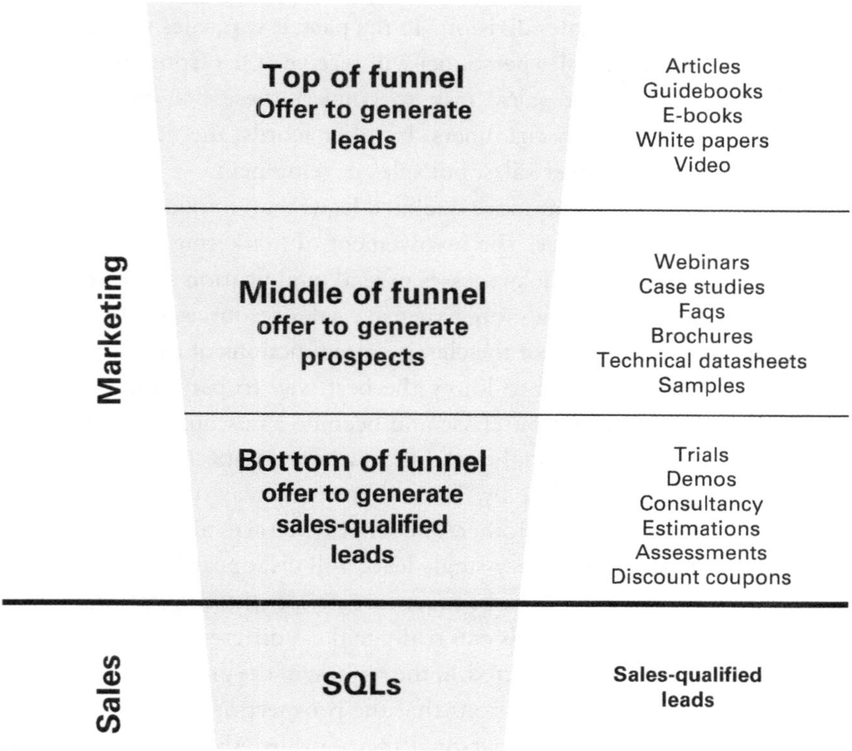

	Top of funnel Offer to generate leads	Articles Guidebooks E-books White papers Video
Marketing	**Middle of funnel** offer to generate prospects	Webinars Case studies Faqs Brochures Technical datasheets Samples
	Bottom of funnel offer to generate sales-qualified leads	Trials Demos Consultancy Estimations Assessments Discount coupons
Sales	**SQLs**	**Sales-qualified leads**

In future, marketing will also be given much more responsibility on the revenue side. As a result, marketing will be regarded less and less as a cost centre and increasingly seen as a revenue driver. However, marketing success or failure will also be judged on the basis of this new responsibility. It will no longer be a question of how many emails have been sent, how many people attended this year's seminars, how many views the latest promotional video has attracted, etc.

Instead, it will be about how many SQLs resulted from those mails, seminars and videos. Or about how many of these leads have been (or still have the potential to be) converted into (long-term) income generation for the company.

As we will see later, modern marketing automation generates metrics that will analyse the return of each individual marketing action at an individual accountability level. Marketing will therefore have information and figures at its disposal that will demonstrate the added value it has created, something that is all too often lacking today. What's more, it will be possible to allocate this added value to specific people and projects.

And what about the sales division? In the past, it was sales who provided the leads. In the future, sales personnel will receive SQLs from their marketing colleagues. It will be sales' task to convert these first into qualified prospects, and finally into customers. In other words, the new function of the salesperson is no longer sales, but sales development.

It is a matter of logic that more qualified leads than unqualified leads will be converted into purchases. The involvement of marketing and, above all, marketing automation in the processes of lead qualification and lead nurturing is cheaper than devoting more expensive sales resources to these tasks.

Having said all this, one of the classic sales functions of the past will still survive. Sales will still need to know the best way to persuade a prospect to actually make their first purchase and become a customer. It will still be salespeople who close the final deal, but in a more respectful and less bullish manner than in days gone by. The old hard-sell way of working will no longer be tolerated by the customer. The seller who races around like a headless chicken, chasing after every single lead, will disappear from the scene.

Modern sales work needs to be more targeted, with sales staff only intervening where their selling skills can really make a difference. They will only make visits when they are expected, at the request of the prospect or customer. Or when there are clear indications that the prospect or customer wants to enter into a deeper and more personal relationship. Above all, the sales of the future will be conducted on the phone, or via Skype, GoToMeeting and social media. It can easily be done at home.

> Sales will only make visits at the request of the customer or when there are clear indications that the customer wants to enter into a deeper and more personal relationship.

As for customer service, there will always be a need for someone to answer the phone and provide customers with the problem-solving support they so badly need. But in the years ahead, there will be much more to customer service than this. Customer service operatives will also need to work proactively and provide tailor-made services to prospects and customers.

Customer service will become the hub of relational management. Every type of media will be used to make this possible: the phone, social media, email, the company website and chat. Like marketing, customer service will no longer be seen as a cost centre, but as an investment in customer loyalty.

> Customer service will become the priority point of contact for prospects and customers, much more so than sales.

Figure 4.5 Infographic: Different ways of dealing with information overload

Frequent users of social media develop different ways of dealing with information overload to other consumers.

1 Digital lifestyle users generally have shortened attention span.

2 Heavy users of social media process many of the online impulses they receive in a superficial manner, alternating with regular but short peaks of heightened attention.

3 Heavy users of social media develop a mental filter that allows them to decide quickly and with minimal stress in which offers they want to invest more time and effort. The rest they just forget.

4 79 percent of frequent social media users are used to working with double screens, whilst simultaneously watching the television, their smartphone and/or their tablet.

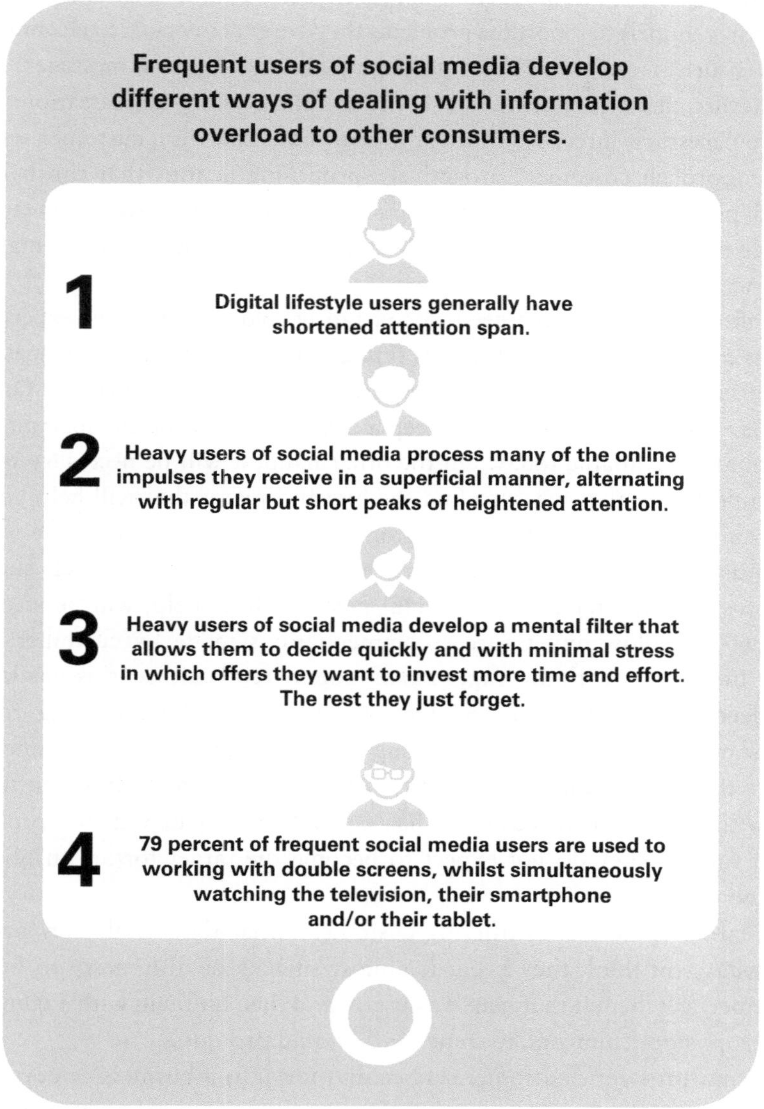

SOURCE Based on data from the National Centre for Biotechnology Information and the National Library of Medicine, USA

In order to maintain an optimum relationship with prospects and customers, accessibility and speed of reaction time are crucial. People will use a variety of different channels to report the problems they are experiencing. Each company must ensure that it is capable of picking up all these different messages.

It is also the task of customer service to follow online conversations and, where necessary, intervene in them in real time. Likewise, customer service must approach customers proactively, proposing actions that can help to avoid problems before they ever arise. To make this possible, customer service needs to be in constant two-way communication with sales, marketing and value delivery.

Online activity and the need to constantly feed the customer experience means that the managing of details (in data, in technology, in messages and in marketing operations) will inevitably become more important[7]. On the one hand, it will be necessary to keep a broad overview of the huge mass of information available today. On the other hand, it will be necessary to dig down deep into that mass, to find the bits and pieces that will help you to do your best for each individual customer.

Statistics are currently circulating in commercial circles which suggest that customers, after receiving useful post-purchase help, will be strongly inclined to follow any future recommendations made by customer desk staff. In markets with an Anglo-Saxon commercial culture, this has led to the development of a questionable line of thought. This thinking argues that staff should use this credit during contact moments with customers to nudge them in the direction of a new or repeat purchase. However, this is not without risk. If the customer has a problem, they expect that problem to be solved. They do not expect to become the target for an unsolicited commercial proposal.

Creating value means offering customers what they think they need – not what you think they need. It almost smacks of dishonesty to help a customer, ask them if that help was useful and then hit them with a commercial proposition, almost like some kind of quid pro quo.

Do not turn your customer service division into a business opportunity. This demonstrates an almost cold-hearted approach to sales and is wholly incompatible with the concept of authenticity. One wrong question at the wrong time could destroy in seconds all the hard-won enchantment you have built up so carefully over months and years. It is almost like pulling a drowning man out of the sea, giving him the kiss of life – and then asking if he would like to buy a new lifejacket from you!

The correct and more warm-hearted approach is to give customers help when they need it, thereby ensuring that their customer experience with your company remains memorable and carefree. This is the best way to indirectly promote future sales, rather than seeing customer service as some kind of backdoor to a more direct sales pitch.

If you still insist on upselling, at least do it honestly and with a little more subtlety, at a moment when you are sure that the customer will be open to such an offer without taking offence.

Table 4.2   A summary of the changes in marketing, sales and customer service

Marketing	Sales	Customer service
Marketing takes responsibility for the management of the sales cycle before, during and after the purchase.	Sales convert sales-qualified leads into qualified prospects and customers	Customer service is the new hub of customer relations management.
Marketing generates leads.	Sales visits become the exception rather than the rule.	Customers are approached proactively with suggestions and action that can help to avoid problems before they arise.
Marketing carries out sales nurturing to allow marketing-qualified leads (MQL) to develop into sales-qualified leads (SQL).	Sales conduct their work via telephone, Skype and social media.	
Marketing is in permanent communication with sales and customer service.	Sales are in permanent communication with marketing and customer service	Customer service is in permanent communication with sales and marketing.

Lead generation

In years gone by, it was always the sales division that generated the leads. This usually happened when sales still needed to earn its place within the organization or in its rare moments of quality time between all the constant travelling to customers and other (spontaneous) prospects. In the meantime, marketing organized mailings and printed brochures for dispatch and distribution.

Marketing was responsible for the company stand at trade fairs and the films that were screened there, as well as (later) the flashy website and the obligatory Facebook page. They also telephoned around to ask if their mailings had been received, following which their colleagues from sales made personal site visits to the companies in question, hoping to arouse their interest.

It was a bit like throwing bait into a fish pond and waiting to see if anyone would bite. The sales staff were always confident that someone would take the bait and after their site visits were even confident that they could predict who it would be. But their 'seller's instinct' was all your company had to go on. What was actually happening in the dark waters beneath the surface of the pond remained a mystery...

It was not exactly a model of efficiency. In fact, it was both costly and time-consuming – and certainly no longer appropriate for today's modern markets. Consider, for example, just one element: the non-stop increase in traffic jams and the growing unwillingness of customers to make time for sales discussions. This means that the number of quality sales visits a sales rep can conduct in a day has been drastically reduced in recent years – with an inevitable impact on overall return.

> You need to be really good to compete for customer attention against all the other spam and noise that is floating around.

You can always opt for an intermediate solution, focusing on telemarketing and the regular distribution of mailings. Unfortunately, however, these techniques are already being practiced on a massive scale, so that they no longer yield the results they once did. In fact, nowadays they more often than not induce an allergic rather than a positive reaction.

You need to be really good to compete for customer attention with your mails and telephone calls against all the other spam and noise that is floating around. What's more, the laws on privacy make it almost impossible to just phone up anyone out of the blue, while too much spamming leads to blacklisting. A red card for inappropriate behaviour.

Lead generation should take place within a fairly strict framework, in which you know which customers are a match for your strategy and which are not. Once you have decided this, it is a question of making contact with the suitable customers, using a gentle approach. In this way, they will be able to form an opinion of your company and your products in a calm and serene manner.

But gentle doesn't mean soft. You still want to make a good and confident first impression. It is only during the next phase that you allow the customer to find the fast track to your organization. Having sufficient creativity to make yourself properly heard against the huge background noise of the marketplace is essential.

Remember that you only get four seconds to breach the customer's barrier of indifference and a further 30 seconds to gain their attention. After that, they will either carry on reading your message – or will classify it in the category 'boring, irrelevant and not worth bothering about'.

Creativity – in ideas, in (graphic) design, in media use, etc – can always make the difference, even with a gentle approach. Marketeers who produce mind-bendingly tedious content, post it on Hootsuite and other efficiency winners, and then keep on rehashing the same turgid nonsense almost *ad infinitum* irritate prospects more than you can imagine. It creates information overload and a general feeling of distrust and reluctance when it comes to commercial messages.

Lead generation starts where your customers are: online.

Lead generation today starts where your customers are: online. This means you will need to ask questions and launch topics on Facebook or LinkedIn, or in other fora where your potential customers are present. For this reason, it is important to identify these fora and the communities in which they are active.

Nowadays, anyone who has a problem can easily 'throw it in the group' online. Prospects will also do this within their own communities. People who share a problem in this way count on others to help them solve that problem. This is one of the benefits of the internet. It therefore makes sense for your company to organize an online listening platform that reacts immediately when prospects ask questions or signal problems. It would also be a good idea to set up a users' group.

Be open to the suggestions and collaboration of your customers. And make sure people see what you are doing – literally. Make good use of photo and video apps like Instagram, Pinterest, Vimeo and YouTube. Also try formats like Snapchat to add a new dynamic to your communication. And don't forget to invest in infographics and other tools that will allow you to make complex matters clear and simple in a fun manner.

Marketing now leads the process of lead generation. It is marketing that offers customers the solutions they are looking for. It is marketing that generates the leads and builds up brand presence in all possible fora. It is marketing that sets up and manages the online instruments that support prospects in their search for answers to their questions. It is marketing that creates the content that customers and prospects find interesting. Classic sales only enters the picture if there is something that marketing cannot easily do online.

Getting new clients via Facebook and Instagram

Back in April 2012, Mark Zuckerberg announced a major milestone in Facebook's history. The company had just paid $1billion in stock and cash in order to add the mobile photo-and-video sharing app Instagram to its portfolio.

Since that moment, both brands have built on their relationship. In the third quarter of 2012, the number of active Facebook users passed a billion, making it the first social network ever to do so[8]. Today, Facebook is by far the most popular social media channel in the world and it envelops the world of social media consumption. With 1.94 billion monthly active users (first quarter 2017[9]), it alone engages a quarter of Earth's human population (cat and dog profiles not included).

Facebook counts 1.23 billion daily active users, of which 1.15 billion are accessing the social media platform using their smartphone[10]. 80 per cent of its revenue is generated via mobile. Add to this the fact that Facebook also owns WhatsApp, Messenger and Instagram, you get an idea of how far their social media empire reaches. The WhatsApp fan base counts 1.2 billion active users. Facebook Messenger adds another 1 billion.

And since inception, Instagram's growth rate has been quite exceptional[11], passing from 1 million users in its early days back in 2010 to reach 600 billion active users in 2017. More and more marketers and businesses develop a presence on Instagram and these numbers continue to grow fast. 2017 saw more than 8 million business profiles on Instagram, increasing about five times since September 2016; it also hits more than a million monthly advertisers[12].

> The combination of Facebook and Instagram needs to be a crucial part of your combined sales and marketing plan.

All of these numbers make your approach towards Facebook and connected photo-and-video apps of pivotal importance. Consider for instance, that online video accounted for 75 per cent of online traffic in 2017; 59 per cent of executives then agree that if both text and video are available on the same topic, they are more likely to prefer the video[13]. This is all vital information for your content plan.

Photo and video sharing platforms are far more personal than simple text platforms. This means business has to shift its brand identity towards a personalized style[14], or an appealing interactive expressive style, relating to the online image consumer.

The most important thing is to get a clear view on the kind of content you want to share. What is its purpose? The content you post must both relate to the users and to your brand, inspiring target users to connect with your values.

Instagram and the photo and video format are ideal to share what your company is all about[15]. That includes things like behind-the-scenes peeks at what your brand is doing to delight customers, customer showcases, success stories, quotes that can inspire customers, humour and games. Add an attractive hashtag, location and time data which links to your content. Insert a call to action.

The ability to share content across multiple platforms with one click is an asset. The most comfortable way to do so is by linking Instagram to Facebook. But be careful. Multitasking on social media can go horribly wrong. To avoid mistakes, it is best to set up both a business Facebook and professional Instagram profile. When you want to combine both platforms content-wise, you have to make sure both platforms are connected in the settings of both social platforms. Once linked, you use 'Share Settings' to determine where you'll be sharing content, for example the pages of your business profile.

The importance of LinkedIn as a sales engine

LinkedIn positions itself as a powerful business networking tool, making it easier than ever before to be more productive and successful. In doing so, it has become widely popular, surviving changing technology and social network fashions. The value of each and every network largely depends on the number and value of relationship knots.

With its number of members steadily growing, showing a double-digit increase each quarter and reaching 500 million in April 2017, LinkedIn is perhaps the major player in the public corporate social media landscape. 40 per cent of members use LinkedIn daily and an average user spends 17 minutes on LinkedIn every month[16].

On LinkedIn, in practice, this generally comes down to people accessing the network to post their CVs, managing their connections and inviting contacts to get connected, publishing stories about points of interest and developing topics in discussion forums.

Across this flowing river of talent, recruiters and head-hunters are increasingly tapping into the network, using the platform in their search for potential candidates. With the advanced search tools on offer they scout for talent, matching specific keywords, and subsequently post job opportunities by InMail. They can join industry or business topic related groups to get more connected. As a result, LinkedIn is widely considered a job or career-related site.

LinkedIn is also a selling system, although it is not widely perceived as such.

Yet LinkedIn is also a selling system, although it is not widely perceived as such. In the age of social media, leveraging a social professional network like LinkedIn to drive sales leads is something to take on board. When adopting with the right strategies and techniques, equipped with the correct mindset, it can become a powerful sales tool.

With its broad range and advanced search and filtering system, LinkedIn enables sales lead generation success by allowing sales professionals to easily and quickly find the right prospects. An interesting statistic: 50 per cent of B2B buyers use LinkedIn as a source for making purchase decisions[17].

LinkedIn advertises its Sales Navigator as support to sales professionals for finding and building relationships with customers and prospects through social selling. The rationale behind this social selling is that the one-to-one approach in selling is becoming less effective. In 2017, a buying decision was influenced by an average of 5.4 decision makers, states LinkedIn[18].

In our era of more flat organizations – self-authorizing agile teams, open iterative decision-making and distributed governance – the one-to-one sales approach is rapidly becoming obsolete, reflecting times of vertical organizations and corresponding hierarchy. Thus, 'sales professionals have to go deeper into the buying team's structure, creating and building many relationships'[19]. LinkedIn's advanced search and filtering system can be used to quickly identify influencers and decision makers and save them as leads to create high quality lead lists.

Sales Navigator is a data driven product, enhancing the efficiency and relevance of the relation between the buyer and yourself. The Sales Navigator tool enables you to get real-time insights on your accounts and leads, including job changes, news mentions, and new potential leads that you had not previously thought about[20]. It generates custom recommendations to discover more people at your target accounts.

Sales Navigator also offers the possibility to unlock the network, enabling you to identify and contact prospects who don't reside in the first three layers of your personal network. The principal reason why organizations using this tool are up to 50 per cent more successful at *converting opportunities into sales results* is that they can rely on the shared network and openly share contact points[21].

LinkedIn offers tremendous opportunities to boost sales. At CPI, LinkedIn business is one of our fastest growing areas.

Sales tips for using LinkedIn

1 Create an effective executive profile

2 Efficiently connect with the people that matter

3 Leverage your mutual connections

4 Find your top tier customers

5 Follow your customers' activity in real-time

6 Listen to conversations and debate

7 Use LinkedIn Pulse to stay on top of industry trends

8 Reach people directly and more credibly with InMail

9 Engage with your customers

10 Publish content

SOURCE LinkedIn, 2017[22]

The social selling approach is all about leveraging one's network to map the 'to be convinced' buying group inside the prospects' organisation and built the necessary number of contact points. 76 per cent of B2B buyers prefer to work with recommendations from their professional network[23]. The introduction through a social network seems to generate some kind of positive psychological effect, which translating itself into a more favourable impression of the salesperson with the customer.

In short, you might be considered less as sales and more as a valuable connection. LinkedIn says that case studies demonstrate leveraging networks for introductions eliminates cold calls and the insights gained from social conversation help to personalize pitches[24].

Of course, the networks exist on both sides. On your side of the virtual corridor, other colleagues may already have developed a connection with the prospect, not with the aim of selling, but offering the opportunity for an introduction into the prospect's decision chart. The TeamLink tool in Sales Navigator uncovers the best ways to get warm introductions with prospects through your company's network.

> The introduction through a social network translates itself into a more favourable impression of the salesperson with the customer.

Lead nurturing, scoring, qualification and conversion

In order to turn a prospect into a customer, it is necessary to create and then deepen a bond of mutual interest. In some cases, this good relationship might not always lead to the placement of many orders. However, it should at the very least yield information about user experience that may be valuable to other potential new customers.

In short, in this new sales era you need to give customers time to evolve from prospecting mode into purchasing mode. But this should not stop you from planning their possible customer journeys, carefully and continually anticipating their wishes and questions. This is not wasted time. It is realistic to expect that this journey – with a little more help and encouragement on your part – will one day be taken.

The art of modern selling is to put your company in the spotlight online, whilst at the same time following your potential customers' activities and gathering further information about them. If you are able to do this, you will be ready to react quickly and effectively when the first live contact is made. Let prospects come to you and wait until the moment arrives when they decide of their own volition to become a customer, before you take a more active role. Until this happens, just keep following, noting their actions.

Thanks to marketing automation, you will know roughly how many times a prospect has visited your website, what they viewed, in what order they viewed it, how long they stayed on each page and what information they downloaded. This will be supplemented by additional details from the different request screens and simulators used. You can also gain insights from the data the prospect left behind whilst surfing on social media and other resource sites, to which the best CRM systems are automatically linked.

This kind of information puts you well ahead in the race to secure that prospect's custom. You know who you are dealing with, so that when the moment for the first direct contact arrives you can immediately focus on pre-identified interests.

You will note that I used the word 'roughly'. I did so deliberately. Digital tracking is fantastic. But it is linked to the IP address of a user or some other identification code of a device used by them. What's more, you need to ask permission to track these interactions. This means that as soon as the prospect or customer visits your site again with a new device, or refuses to accept your cookies, you temporarily lose track of them and your touchpoint registration will no longer be accurate.

Fortunately, most people nowadays work with two or three devices. They also tend to accept cookies more or less automatically. As a result, you will quickly get back on the scent of their digital footprint, making it possible for you to follow the majority of their interactions. This is much better than in the past, when – without tracking technology – you were just groping in the dark.

But there is a downside. When the use of tracking becomes more commonplace, prospects and customers will receive an ever-increasing amount of 'spontaneous' offers and information. It is only to be expected that they then will become more selective about who they will allow to accompany them on their customer journey. This selectivity will probably find expression in a growing refusal to accept cookies and tracking. Prospects and customers will systematically install ad-blockers or tools like Clutter.

As a result, mails that do not correspond with the customer's self-programmed reading behaviour will automatically be classified as unimportant – and probably not be read.

This means that in future you will need to display a good deal of originality if you want to be admitted to your customer's inner circle. Content bombardment is guaranteed to fail. Gone are the days when you could send the same message every two hours to fifteen different platforms with the simple click of a mouse. This approach will no longer work, which signals the end for the old-style marketeers who put quantity before quality.

The new buzz term is *lead nurturing*, the feeding of leads with nice bite-sized chunks of added value. Step by step. If a contact shows that they are interested in a particular subject – for example, by downloading a white paper (which will give you their email address) – you can approach them spontaneously, perhaps by sending an invitation to a webinar or an informal suggestion to watch one of your videos. Once again, click behaviour will be monitored.

If the prospect reacts positively to your initiative, this can be taken as a sign of growing engagement. Each positive signal, like additional pages read or questions asked, provides you with further profile information and profile points for the development of further initiatives.

The points that you register in this manner will allow you to give the lead a score. On the basis of this lead score, you can automatically trigger a number of additional actions and/or tasks. Prospects and customers with a high lead score soon appear on the radar of sales and customer service, so that they can be followed up in the most appropriate manner. The failure to receive further positive signals my result in the lead score being reduced.

In this way, you can systematically move your prospects through the conversion funnel. The intention is to generate as many qualified leads as possible, but without immediately launching into something that resembles a sales trajectory.

Lead nurturing: the nature of the beast

The nature of the information and the medium in which the prospect is interested can tell you a great deal about which phase of the journey they are currently following as a potential customer. As they gradually move towards the purchase phase, they will become more open to different content.

This also applies to the way that content is packaged. These evolutions make it possible to assess the prospect's changing level of engagement. Marketing automation is vital in this process, with its ability to constantly monitor your contacts' click and surf behaviour, reactions to emails, the completion of online forms, etc.

Figure 4.6   Generating qualified leads – which techniques are most successful?

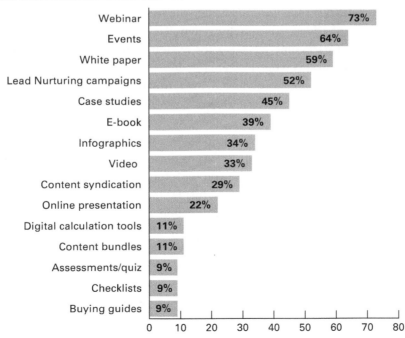

SOURCE 2015 Demand Gen Report Benchmark Study

Figure 4.7   Converting contacts into customers – which techniques are most successful?

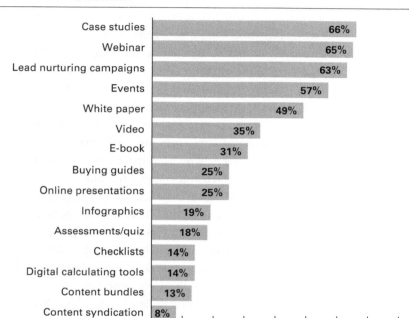

SOURCE 2015 Demand Gen Report Benchmark Stud

The customer will probably suspect that you are collecting information about them. But this need not necessarily be a source of irritation. After all, you are required to inform visitors if you are using cookies on your website. Moreover, the use of cookies has become more or less standard practice, which most consumers nowadays accept without worrying about it. Nor is there any reason why they should. After all, they get something in return: inspiration in exchange for information.

Lead qualification is essential if you want to develop leads or prospects into customers. Remember that not every lead will ultimately result in a customer relationship. The traditional practice of distributing and collecting visiting cards at a trade fair, perhaps attracted by a special fair price, seldom produces really interested leads. You can immediately forget about most of them (chance visitors, students, competitors, etc).

A more limited number of others will be serious about your product, while the intentions of a third group will be less clear but still potentially interesting. It is the task of the marketing division to separate the wheat from the chaff and to decide when a lead actually becomes sales-ready.

It is the task of marketing to decide when a lead actually becomes sales-ready.

When marketing hands over the leads to the sales department, it is the latter's task to guide the customer towards the purchase. But sales must continue to keep marketing informed about the success or failure of the lead conversion. In this way, marketing will know which of its various initiatives/ actions are most effective, so that its marketing programme can be more finely tuned. This exchange of information takes place via the CRM and via automatically generated marketing and sales performance reports.

If a trade fair results in a large number of leads, but if few or none of them are afterwards converted into customers, it is open to question whether future attendance at this particular fair serves any real purpose. The same principle can be applied to a Google Adwords campaign. If, after six months, you have had plenty of leads but no customers, pull the plug.

In the years ahead, sales will be much less focused on the generation of leads, concentrating instead on lead conversion. This will largely be done on the basis of contact via email and telephone. Much of the outgoing communication can be automated. Even the final conclusion of the purchase can also be arranged online. In this new configuration, the telephone becomes a lifeline for those who get bogged down in the automated process. As already mentioned, customer visits will become something of a rarity: the exception rather than the rule.

These considerations lead logically to a further question: is it possible to any longer justify the organizational sub-division between internal and external services? If a lead is converted into a customer via a fully automated online system, no further intervention is really required. The deal is concluded automatically and the data relating to the sale is automatically recorded and processed.

If it is still necessary to do something by telephone, the time spent will be similarly registered and analysed. And if – very exceptionally – a site visit is requested or required, automatic checks will first be made to see if this expensive mode of acquisition can be justified in financial terms, based on a prognosis of the likelihood of success.

Value delivery

Value delivery relates to the entire process through which you manage the relationship with customers by promising and ultimately providing them with value. This is not simply a question of the value represented by a product or service, but is also about the way you communicate, the way you respect agreements, the way you listen, the way you understand your customers' needs, the way you take on board their advice and allow them to help in the development of appropriate solutions.

Later, it is also about making things as easy as possible for customers to maintain the relationship: by providing them with tools that allow them to make their wishes known quickly and simply, by responding to these wishes promptly, by managing data and administration carefully, by being constantly available via a hotline, helpdesk or chat-box, by developing clear customer pages, downloads and customer specification sheets, etc.

Customers are always on the look-out for the most efficient and effective way to achieve their objectives. This means that every unnecessary delay and obstacle can lead to frustration. What customers want is 'simpler, easier and cheaper'.

Companies usually wait until a customer has signalled a need before they respond with a value offer. The initiative in the relationship is left to the customer: for example, by phoning for information or placing an order. In short, the customer acts first. This has been made even easier by the internet. The customer goes online, finds the order page and places an order. It is almost a DIY process: customers serve themselves, fill their shopping basket, check out and pay. In the company, these details are automatically processed, the order is put together and the delivery sent.

Nowadays, most suppliers are already monitoring the use and stock evolution of their customers. Suppliers now remind their customers when their stocks are running low and in some cases even automatically initiate repeat orders. This also makes possible the better management of your own stock levels and production. In exchange for this sharing of information, the customer expects to receive solutions for problems and needs that have not yet arisen.

Customer feedback

It is the customer's experience that counts. Consequently, all feedback from the customer is important. Even feedback that is not initially directed at your company. The systematic capture and correct analysis of customer feedback is crucial. In this way, you can discover whether your product or service actually provides the value you have promised in the perception of the customer.

This also gives you the opportunity, if necessary, to adjust your offer on the basis of the information received before your relationship sours or is even terminated altogether.

All feedback from the customer is important, even if it is not initially directed at your company.

But customer feedback does more than simply tell you whether or not you are on the right track, allowing you to estimate that customer's likely future value. It is also a lever that can help you when it comes to rewarding your own personnel. If you ask your customers about the quality of their recent experiences with your company, and if you further ask them whether or not they would be prepared to recommend your product or service, you can link their answers to the trajectory they have followed through your organization. In other words, you can trace their responses to specific members of staff.

This makes the connection between satisfaction and approach transparent. This method is already applied in both retail and B2B, and is a huge stimulus for companies to make the customer central to everything they do.

Management and control

Management and control go together. This has always been the case. In the past, however, this involved a large element of guesswork. Sales managers made predictions and targets were set. But because there was a lack of intermediate information about the progress being made – in other words, how the customers were evolving – huge pressure was placed on the sellers. They needed to make their figures – at all costs.

The sales books were run according to the principles of man-loading and span of control, concepts that were adopted from the military sphere: how many customers and regions can we place on the shoulders of single salesperson? The object of control was to load this salesperson with folders and samples and then launch them at the customers, with the instruction not to come back until targets had been hit. As a result, customers were also bombarded with products, not all of which they wanted or needed.

In today's markets, formal hierarchical structures and processes aimed at pure control increasingly need to give way to community-driven organizations. This is happening because people nowadays are better educated and often already know the best way to approach things. They don't like to have the company looking over their shoulder, telling them what to do. A modern sales organization now needs to work with self-steering teams. Staff manage themselves and organize their own activities within clearly defined fields of competence.

This flexibility makes it difficult to talk in terms of a 'span of control'. Instead, there is a span of loose interactions and alliances[25].

A modern sales organization now needs to work with self-steering teams.

This means that we expect a new style of leadership from the 21st century sales manager. It is no longer necessary to monitor and follow up the activities of the individual sellers and teams. It has become more a question of enabling those individuals and teams. How? By developing processes that allow people to work in an autonomous and relaxed way and by providing them with instruments that can show them how well they are doing. Today's sales manager also needs to focus more on forging strategic alliances with partners, which will make it possible to generate increased sales by surfing on the same wave as others.

Are targets a thing of the past? No, they are not. Targets still need to be set, but as part of a collaborative process that involves all concerned. The challenge of the organization is to maintain its focus, channelling its talent in the right direction towards excellent results. This will not be possible with rules, control mania and the imposition of the heavy hand of authority. It will only be achieved by creating the best possible conditions for a well-motivated and well-trained workforce.[26]

In broad terms, the agreed targets still need to be linked to task allocation, follow-up and feedback. But the targets themselves are no longer plucked out of thin air. The days of 'Here is your monthly target, now get on with it!' are a thing of the past. Each target is now framed within a process that will help to make the reaching of the target possible. Members of staff are constantly provided with new information that allows them to self-adjust their actions and behaviour.

Task assignment, as the name implies, involves the allocation of particular tasks to particular members of staff on the basis of a number of predetermined criteria. Task assignment guarantees that the available resources will be used in the most purposeful manner. Everyone does what they do best. This will allow the organization to be structured so that there are sufficient people to generate leads, convert leads and deliver value.

Like target setting, follow-up will continue to be necessary. It is only common sense to keep a finger on the pulse of your commercial organization. However, this finger can be held much more lightly and much more easily than in the past. Nowadays, the technology exists to monitor unobtrusively matters such as average order size, the percentage of repeat orders, the extent to which customers follow their historical or predicted order rhythm, and so on.

These technological aids are more than necessary, because it is no longer simply a question of monitoring your commercial operations in isolation. You now also need to monitor how customers experience their relationship with your product and your company throughout the entire length of their customer journey.

Marketing automation and CRM generate automatically and in real time a series of metrics that chart the quality of this relationship, and visualize the results in an easy-to-read dashboard. The feedback provided by the system makes it possible to correct deviations from the planned trajectory and suggest possibilities to further enhance the customer experience.

In this respect, there is a crucial difference with the salesperson of yesteryear. Information about performance is more than a series of figures about the number of visits, the number of leads and the number of conversions to sales. It is also about the way value is delivered to the customer within an agreed framework.

As a result, metrics relating to on-time delivery, full delivery, net promoter score (NPS), speed of problem-solving response and so on are now systematically included in the dashboards, so that, for example, it is possible to see how many prospects terminated their customer journey, at which stage, and why.

Continuous improvement

The objective is clear: to continually do things better and better. It sounds great as a slogan, doesn't it? But how do you actually turn it into reality? To make things better, you first need to know where they are going wrong – and for what reason.

It is not just about improving the quality of the value you provide, but also about effectively transferring that value to the customer. In other words, it is about customer satisfaction.

You will be able to achieve this continual improvement thanks to the data provided by your management and control systems and the input received from your customers and staff. The feedback of customers, their reactions to the things you propose, their suggestions and ideas will all help you to assess what they find important and what they find irrelevant. If customers think you are providing something that is not important to them, they will not be prepared to pay for it.

Input from your staff is necessary to assess the static information produced by the metrics and to channel the energy derived from this information into increased efficiency and effectiveness. The crucial metrics are automatically generated by the system. But the opinions of the customer and your staff are anything but automatic. As a result, you not only need to make it easy for customers to provide feedback, but must also invite them regularly to do so. You must systematically listen to the VOC: the voice of the customer.

How can you do this? One way, for example, is to invite customers to take part in online discussions or workshops. Sometimes, this can be organized in the form of a game (gamification), so that the provision of information also provides the customer with a new experience.

The same applies to staff. You involve them by making it easy for them to express their opinions. But you also need to tell them what you have done with their feedback. Nothing is more frustrating for an employee than to be asked for an opinion, only to discover later that it has not been listened to. This does not, of course, mean that you must automatically follow staff opinions to the letter. But it does mean that you need to explain what you are doing and why, particularly when you have decided not to act on certain ideas or comments.

By asking for staff feedback in this manner, your people will feel more attached to the organization and be better able to recognize their place in it. They will experience that their field of responsibility extends beyond their own function. In the new world of sales, maintaining the customer relationship is the task of everyone in the company. Consequently, it is important to give everyone the possibility to make their own personal contribution, no matter how small.

In this respect, training and re-education play a crucial role. Training should ideally be organized on a modular basis via a platform that makes possible on-demand learning. This type of platform allows employees to log in to a learning system, where they can choose a particular course of instruction to follow. These courses can be developed, for example, around a series of short films or cartoons that highlight certain concepts. Preferably, they should include a number of interactive elements in which the trainee needs to apply these concepts.

It is also useful to have an evaluation test at the end to ensure that the relevant lessons have been properly learnt. Training of this kind should also be extended beyond your own staff, to include any intermediary companies and their personnel. In this way, some companies that sell their products via do-it-yourself stores train the staff in these stores through films that can be accessed via a QR code on the packaging of the product.

Talent development

Companies need to redefine the roles of marketing, sales and customer service. This will require the learning and use of new skills. Marketing, sales and customer service will become more and more like sciences. As a result, the staff working within this new organization will need to be authentic, accountable and agile.

We will increasingly hear the call: 'Ring out the old, ring in the new!'

In the years ahead, many jobs will disappear and new ones will be created. More people will leave the labour market than will join it. It will not be possible to solve all your problems simply by attracting the right new people, but new people will certainly be necessary to change the things that need to be changed. We will increasingly hear the call: 'Ring out the old, ring in the new!'

Every decision needs to be tested against a control factor. And once control is involved, it immediately becomes necessary to check whether that control is really required. Perhaps it obstructs more than it solves? Every decision also needs to be weighed against its possible impact on levels of trust within the organization.

This trust is vital. Without it, the exchange between more personal freedom in the job and greater personal responsibility for measurable results can never be made to work. Trust is also necessary to facilitate smooth working between staff of different generations. It is important to engage all staff of whatever age by allowing them to participate in the discussions about individual objectives and key results. Let them make decisions about the kind of tools and devices they want to use. Help those who can't decide for themselves. Be constantly on your guard against accepting things simply because 'that's the way we've always done it'.

I am certain that your organization possesses considerable commercial and marketing talent. That's the good news. The bad news is that this talent often hides itself away. You need to find out why, where they are – and do something about it.

Once again, training is very important in this respect. Skills, competencies and market insights require continual updating through forms of blended learning, which involves a mix of classical and online teaching methods. In our fast-moving modern world, it is crucial to remain abreast of the latest developments. And companies that wish to introduce the most recent state-of-the-art technology must remember that time and effort is also necessary to learn how to use it properly.

Commercial organizations need to become learning organizations, with well-considered personal learning for each employee. It is important that these employees can both follow a fixed curriculum (for example, as part of their onboarding) and be invited for specific training that is particularly relevant for them. This will obviously require an investment to be made: to help people unlearn old habits, to train them in new skills, to discover their hidden talents, etc.

But in exchange for this investment the staff concerned must be willing to take greater responsibility. This must provide a future return for the company in terms of greater efficiency, fewer layers of management and better overall financial results.

With regard to marketing automation, most suppliers offer adequate training as part of their package. This usually includes classic workshops, webinars, seminars, etc. Successful completion usually results in the participant being awarded a certificate, and I have often noted the effort that people are prepared to make to get such a certificate. And with good reason – because this increases their market value. There is also more specific training for matters such as dealing with big data or the integration of technology.

Of course, none of this is cheap. The price of a good classic course in a renowned training institute can quickly run into thousands of euros. But it is usually worth it because it bears repeating: good training is more important than ever. And it is equally important to link it as closely as possible to best market practice.

A good example in this respect is the Beeckestijn Business School. Founded in 1992 by Egbert-Jan Van Bel and Hans Molenaar, it has since grown to become the reference for post-doctoral market training in the Netherlands. Beeckestijn offers specialized courses in the practical application of social and digital approaches to customer care and the use of marketing analytics. It works with only the very best lecturers in the business and academic worlds.

Figure 4.8   Beeckestijn Business School, The Netherlands

In a similar manner, the Vlerick Leuven/Ghent Management School responds to the need in Belgium to train and retrain the sales and marketing gurus of the future. They offer a series of sales conferences and webinars, as well as both short-term and long-term courses. My friend Professor Deva Rangarajan has played a leading role in this project, in particular through his role in the development of the Vlerick Sales Competence Centre.

At an international level, there is a wide range of high-quality training options, offering the latest in-depth insights into the art of disruptive selling. Alongside the classic institutions with well-established and well-deserved reputations, like the Kellogg Business School in the US, Cranfield University in the UK and the Toulouse Business School in France, there are also several new and inspiring platforms. One of these is Crowd Sourcing Week (www.crowdsourcingweek.com), which organizes worldwide inspiration days on themes that include new business models, the sharing economy and crowd-based economics.

Ensuring that your staff are properly trained means more than simply following a course or two – and then forgetting about them. It is about mixing the right number of courses with the right amount of permanent follow-up and refresher training in various fields, preferably with a little international experience thrown in. This will expand the vision of your staff and serve as a source of lasting inspiration.

The day of the lifelong job has gone and will never return. Organizations will need to recruit new talent more frequently than in the past, but on demand and only for the length of time that they need them. Moreover, they will be offered more variable rewards. These will be based on their level of personal development, the extent to which individual and/or group objectives have been reached and the measured levels of customer satisfaction resulting from their activities.

On the other side of the coin, more and more professionals will want to decide for themselves who they work for, when and where – and only for as long as it remains interesting or challenging.

It is up to employers to make sure that these last two criteria are fulfilled. Companies need to develop self-strengthening concepts that create a link between happy customers and happy employees. These are concepts in which each action contributes to the improvement of the present or future operation of the organization. In this way, you will not only take care of today, but also have an eye on tomorrow.

Notes

1 Maes, Patrick (2013) *Sales 3.0*, CPI-Consulting
2 Maes, 2013
3 Maes, 2013
4 Van Belleghem, S (2014) *When Digital Becomes Human: Klantenrelaties in transformatie*, LannooCampus, Leuven

5   Economist Intelligence Unit [accessed Dec 2017] The rise of the marketeer: driving engagement, experience and revenue, *Marketo* [Online] https:// uk.marketo.com/analyst-and-other-reports/the-rise-of-the-marketer- driving-engagement-experience-and-revenue/

6   The marketing team will need to provide different content for a lead who is still at the TOp of the sales FUnnel compared to a lead who has already given some indication of their needs and preferences, and is therefore already in the Middle Of the FUnnel, or a lead who is getting close to making a purchase and is therefore at the BOttom of the FUnnel).

7   Economist Intelligence Unit [accessed Dec 2017]

8   Statista [accessed May 2017] Number of monthly active Facebook users worldwide as of 1st quarter 2017 (in millions) [Online] https://www.statista. com/statistics/264810/number-of-monthly-active-facebook-users-worldwide/

9   Statista [accessed May 2017]

10   Flynn, Kerry [accessed May 2017] Facebook is within reach of 2 billion users, *Mashable* [Online] http://mashable.com/2017/02/01/facebook-earnings- record-user-growth/

11   Parkinson, Gary [accessed May 2017] Facebook Acquires Instagram: 5 Years Later, *Shutterstock Custom* [Online] http://custom.shutterstock.com/blog/ facebook-acquires-instagram-5-years-later

12   Chaykowski, Kathleen [accessed May 2017] Instagram Hits 1 Million Advertisers, Fueled By Small Businesses, *Forbes* [Online] https://www. forbes.com/sites/kathleenchaykowski/2017/03/22/ instagram-hits-1-million-advertisers-fueled-by-small-businesses

13   Insivia [accessed May 2017] 27 Video Stats For 2017 [Online] http:// www.insivia.com/27-video-stats-2017/

14   Parkinson [accessed May 2017]

15   HubSpot [accessed May 2017] How to use Instagram for business [Online] https://offers.hubspot.com/instagram-for-business

16   Aslam, Salman [accessed May 2017] Linkedin by the Numbers: Stats, Demographics & Fun Facts, *Omnicore* [Online] https://www.omnicoreagency. com/linkedin-statistics/

17   LinkedIn Sales Solutions [accessed May 2017] Ultimate Guide to Sales Prospecting: Tips, Techniques and Tools [Online] https://business.linkedin.com/ sales-solutions/b2b-sales-prospecting/techniques-for-successful-prospecting

18   LinkedIn Sales Solutions [accessed May 2017] Ultimate Guide to Sales Prospecting

19   LinkedIn Sales Solutions [accessed May 2017] Getting Started with Social Selling on LinkedIn [Online] https://business.linkedin.com/sales-solutions/ social-selling/getting-started-with-social-selling-on-linkedIn-ebook

20   Altman, Ian [accessed May 2017] LinkedIn Paid Vs Free - A Review Of Sales Navigator, *Forbes* [Online] https://www.forbes.com/sites/ ianaltman/2015/09/01/linkedin-paid-vs-free-a-review-of-sales-navigator/

21 Van der Blom, Richard [accessed May 2017] Hoe social selling de inkoper gelukkig maakt - LinkedIn's Sales Navigator, *marketingfacts.nl* [Online] http://www.marketingfacts.nl/berichten/hoe-social-selling-de-inkoper-gelukkig-maakt-linkedins-sales-navigator

22 LinkedIn Sales Solutions [accessed May 2017] Top 10 Actionable Sales Tips [Online] https://business.linkedin.com/sales-solutions/social-selling/top-10-sales-tips-tricks

23 LinkedIn Sales Solutions [accessed May 2017] Ultimate Guide to Sales Prospecting

24 LinkedIn Sales Solutions [accessed May 2017] Getting Started with Social Selling on LinkedIn

25 Hindle, T [accessed May 2017] Span of control, *The Economist* [Online] http://www.economist.com/node/14301444

26 Vandendriessche, F, and Looten, H (2014) *Leidinggeven Zonder Cijfers: Van input naar output*, LannooCampus, Leuven

Exploring automation and technology for disruptive selling

05

If you want to make your customers happy and keep them happy in the modern marketplace, you need to think about more than just sales. You need to develop a whole new commercial organization. Marketing technology and marketing automation can play a facilitating role in this transformation. Nowadays, these intelligent systems make it possible to automatically follow the process of customer expectation right up to the moment of delivery and even beyond. This is crucial if you hope to turn customers into money-spinning ambassadors.

Why marketing automation?

To provide customers with excellent value at every stage of their customer journey, it is necessary to ensure that sales, marketing and customer service interact with each other seamlessly. Every action by the customer, both online or offline, can be a signal requiring a reaction on your part. To assess each opportunity accurately and develop the right response, you need to monitor and analyse the customer's every move. Will they leave the loyalty loop or stay put? Or are there indications that they might be contemplating a switch at a later stage? If so, what is the best way to react? Or is no reaction the best reaction – for the time being?

These are difficult questions to answer, all the more so because you need to do it in real time. In fact, it is impossible without the assistance of far-reaching automation.

Marketing is essentially the same as sales, but on a much larger scale. Sellers like to give 30-minute presentations in the boardroom. Marketeers transform the same content into a 30-minute webinar or a talk for an entire congress. Marketeers communicate their message to thousands via social media; sellers communicate their message to individuals via the phone. Customer service operatives take care of customers by answering questions and giving the most practical possible expression to that content and message.

All three divisions – marketing, sales and customer service – work within the same trajectory: the development of a relationship with a prospect, who they hope to convert into a satisfied long-term customer.

Yet while marketing, sales and customer service all have the same objective, they use different tools to achieve it. Nowadays, CRM functions primarily as an instrument for sales. The idea behind CRM is that the recording of detailed information about every (possible) customer will keep the seller informed about their needs and wishes, and therefore about their current position in the sales funnel. It is certainly useful for a salesperson to know all these things. But this is insufficient data for a marketeer.

CRM and marketing automation complement each other

CRM provides valuable support for about 30 per cent of the real sales process. This 30 per cent relates primarily to the phase in which there is actual contact between the (potential) customer and the sales team. The information generated by these contacts is stored in the CRM system. However, the remaining 70 per cent of the customer journey nowadays largely takes place online and therefore does not appear on the CRM radar. That part of the trajectory can only be followed with marketing automation and its associated tools.

The integration of CRM and marketing automation provides both sales and marketing with access to information generated at the start of the customer journey. Marketing automation provides automatically and continuously updated information throughout the remainder of the journey. This makes it possible to pass on to sales qualified contacts with a better chance of customer conversion.

The combination of CRM and marketing automation leads on average to a higher ROI of 14.5 per cent on marketing investments in any given project, and each 10 per cent improvement in access to information results in a 14 per cent increase in turnover.[1]

What does marketing automation make possible?

Marketing automation software makes it possible to follow the activity (and non-activity) of the customer throughout the entire length of the customer journey. This immediately has the advantage that your staff no longer need to do this tiresome and time-consuming work. But that is just the start. Marketing automation also makes it possible to collect and collate consumer data from a wide range of online sources. Once combined and automatically analyzed, this data can be used to give a customer profile to every single contact.

In addition, each profile can then be approached via the medium – email, social media or online advertising – and with the message the data suggests is most likely to stimulate movement further through the sales funnel. This might, for example, be a special promotional price, an invitation to a product demo, or a pointer to an interesting conversation.

Marketing automation, as the name implies, also allows you to generate and send these messages automatically. This saves you valuable time, while ensuring that the (potential) customer can receive the information in real time or, alternatively, at a later date (if the system decides that this is a better course of action).

Real time can also mean the setting in motion of a chain of actions that can be spread over a longer period. As a matter of course, these actions – email, online adverts, etc – are tailored to the individual customer's needs, based on their interests and patterns of behaviour online.

But the automated system then takes things yet another stage further. It registers and evaluates which actions and content elicit a good, average or poor response from the targets. The good ones are continued, the poor ones are ditched and the average ones can be held for further consideration. In this way, marketing automation allows the more accurate measuring of relative success and failure. It makes it possible to quantify the impact of a campaign or action, ensuring an optimum focus of effort and resources in the future. This was always difficult to prove in the past, which explains why marketing was often the first target when cuts needed to be made.

The digital footprint left by the customer makes it possible to develop a sales approach tailor-made to that particular customer.

If you permanently have at your disposal the most current information about your customers and their search behaviour, because they themselves are constantly updating this data through their own actions online; if you know when a customer is most likely to open and read their emails; if you know what they are likely to click on and likely to avoid; if you know all these things, you can refine your commercial approach significantly. The content and the timing of this approach can be made to reflect the customer's profile and segment.

As a result, customers not only receive information that interest them, but also at the moment when they are most receptive to it – all because of the traceable details they have left online. These preferences can then be linked to other big data that is available to the organization.

The digital footprint left by the customer therefore makes it possible to develop a tailor-made sales approach, specific to that particular customer. In this way, a general approach can be transformed into micro- and nano-marketing, ultimately resulting in a 'segment of one', the most individual approach of all.

The headache called CRM

When you hear me praising the virtues of marketing automation in this way, perhaps this may remind you of similar talk some years ago about the 'miracle' that was customer relationship management (CRM). Unfortunately, the practical application of this miracle turned out to be flawed in many ways. Nowadays, the mere mention of CRM causes frowns in many companies, if not open hostility. For this reason, it is worth pausing to consider why the implementation of CRM was not always as successful as everyone had hoped.

To begin with, it is never enough simply to drop a new system into an organization. The basis of success lies in working with it effectively. But people need to be motivated to work with it. This will only be the case when it makes their life easier. In other words, it is necessary to engage the people for whom the system is intended. They need to have their say about what the system can and should do. If an innovation makes things simple, it will be accepted more readily and people will be more willing to learn how to use it.

If a system does not work well or is not used, this is often because it is too complicated. The old CRM was indeed complex: poor interfaces, difficult settings, bad connections, and an excess of procedures, flows and boxes that meant nothing to anyone.

The efficient working of any system begins with the mapping of the wishes and expectations of the people who will use it. This involves much more than just checking how the current sales cycle of the company can be linked to the cycle that is installed as standard in the system. Instead, it should involve the design of the perfect sales cycle that the company ideally wants for itself, so that the system can then be designed to best reflect and support this. If there is no internal consensus and clear agreements, the system will copy and emphasize this human indecisiveness.

But let's return to CRM and the headaches it caused. To successfully implement CRM, three preconditions need to be met.

Firstly, the system needs to make new things possible. It needs to enable people. In particular, the system needs to help the commercial organization of the company to profile prospects and customers, to plan a mix of actions at the right moments, and to monitor all relevant touchpoints. If the system fails to do this, there are a number of possible reasons. Perhaps there is something wrong with the profiling of your customers. Or maybe your action planning is too limited, only going as far as setting a date for the next telephone call or meeting. It could be that the contacts monitored are only sales contacts, so that they are insufficiently complete to make the analyses you need. Or else the system is geared to the wishes of one key user, so that it is too complicated for other average users.

Secondly, the system needs to be user-friendly. Not just for the people who use it daily, but for everyone. There are no excuses here. CRM must be intuitive. You must be able to use it without the need for long and complex training. Such training as there is must ensure that everyone has the same understanding of the different boxes and their underlying concepts, and that everyone can extract the information from the system that is important for him or her.

Interfaces that are tiresome to use are automatically used less, often leading to delayed input. If this delay results in old data being added to the system, your CRM will no longer be up-to-date, which significantly reduces its effectiveness. When this happens, the system will soon come to be seen as nothing more than an obligation – a pain in the ass – rather than as a useful support tool.

Thirdly, there must be good linkage with enterprise resource planning (ERP) and other relevant sources of information. When do staff consult the CRM? Only if the information is correct and up-to-date. This sounds logical, yet many CRM systems are constantly struggling to keep up with the flow of incoming data. But it is only when the system is kept fully up-to-date with new and reliable information that it becomes stronger and more useful. Systems that no longer reflect current realities are seldom used. It is much easier to keep key data in your own notebook or to get the right information by calling a contact. This decommissioning of the official CRM system can only be avoided if it is correctly linked to both the company's ERP and marketing automation systems, preferably in real time.

The most important success factor for successful CRM implementation is a good specification of people's expectations. This involves more than simply listing these expectations in a neat file. It also implies the need to make flow charts for matters such as lead generation, customer management, complaint management, the design of screens and reports, and – last but not least – the detailed simulation of user conditions: in the car, in the customer's office, at home in front of the television, on the train, in a plane, on holiday, with or without decent internet access.

> The look-and-feel and the user interface of CRM are just as important as the accuracy of the data it contains.

CRM is a work in progress. This does not mean that you constantly need to fiddle with the basic structure, but you will need to regularly create new fields, design new reports and new functionalities, as well as removing the old and outdated ones. If you have new elements tested and reviewed by the users and their colleagues once or twice a year, this should help you to guard against the possible ageing of your system.

Of course, things are not standing still in the world of CRM; there are new evolutions all the time. Some suppliers such as SalesFlare and Nimble offer a total new approach to CRM solutions, by combining a number of different functionalities. SalesFlare is based on the tracing and prioritizing of mails for the development of a sales pipeline management system that brings artificial intelligence within the reach of SMEs. Nimble makes it possible to connect contacts with LinkedIn profiles, quickly and easily.

Choosing the right partner for the implementation of your CRM is another key factor for success. In recent years, I have monitored more than 35 CRM implementations at close range. A number of the providers were genuine enablers and models of efficiency. Others were little short of a nightmare!

The most successful projects were resolutely driven by the company itself, with the sales and marketing divisions taking the lead. The least successful projects were run by central IT departments, who placed the emphasis on security and integration with other systems, rather than on the day-to-day support of the sales process.

Successful CRM implementations start with an update of this sales process and a critical analysis of the company's current commercial approach. If you overlook this phase, you will end up automating an approach that is outdated, depriving your new CRM of the opportunity to increase your productivity and improve your customer relations.

Basic functionalities

Marketing automation tools usually offer the following five basic functionalities or applications:

1 they make possible the monitoring of online behaviour;
2 they have an email marketing function;
3 they enable customer relationship and contact management;
4 they automate routine functions;
5 they give access to a selection of lead-nurturing and analysis tools.

Most of the marketing automation solutions on the market offer comparable tools. Some packages have a more specific positioning and offer more specific services. For example, they might focus on ecommerce (SALESManago) or content management and the monitoring of blogs (HubSpot). Others are based on native links with specific CRM systems, like Pardot with Salesforce, Click-Dimensions with Microsoft and SilverPop with Sugar CRM.

A few of the large and well-established players in the market, such as the pioneers Marketo and Eloqua, can be linked to every system. In addition, there is a wide range of well-known and not-so-well-known marketing automation packages, which can provide the necessary level of support for companies working in an SME environment.

It may be useful to look at the most common functionalities one by one. In particular, to draw a distinction between the functionalities found in every basic package and the extras, which are only found in the more sophisticated versions, often as exclusive options.[2]

Monitoring of online behaviour

One of the basic features of every marketing automation platform is the ability to identify the people who visit your website, to monitor the time that they spend there, to record what pages they view, and to identify the source that brought them to your site in the first place.

A number of packages give the option to link marketing automation with IP identification. This identification is sometimes further enriched with other information about the customer, such as the names of the managers and their LinkedIn pages. To date, this function works well in the larger markets, where it is sometimes interesting for data suppliers to set up this kind of interaction. In the US, the linking of market automation to identification based on IP addresses is already fairly common, although this is not yet the case in Belgium and the Netherlands (although better in the latter than the former).

Most systems also make it possible to extract additional information, such as the search terms used by your contacts online or the details of their like, share and comment behaviour. Another more advanced function is the ability to monitor the behaviour of your contacts on their mobile devices, which in most cases tells you when the device was used, by whom, where they were located at the time and what they did.

Nowadays, good marketing automation software generally contains social analytics tools that allow you to check what your contacts are saying on social media. The tools can also identify which elements of the content you have sent to your contacts have been shared with others, and who those others are.

It is also feasible to link your marketing automation to, say, Facebook, which allows you to collect profiling information that you can combine with the similar information you have already collected from other sources. However, this latter function is usually an optional extra, for which you have to pay more.

Email marketing

An email function is now standard in the large majority of market automation packages. Mails continue to be one of the best methods for interacting with prospects and guiding them with added value through each phase of the customer journey. Professional packages offer at least the possibility to send emails to a segmented public, linked to the secondary possibility of personalizing the form of address.

Other common features include a spam test, confirmation that the mail has been received by the contact, confirmation whether or not the mail has been opened, and confirmation whether or not it has been re-clicked at a later stage.

Further basic features include the ability to generate and send mails automatically after a contact has exhibited a pre-determined type of behaviour. This might be the filling in of a form or the downloading a particular paper. Alternatively, the system can send a refresher mail if the contact has not visited your site for some time.

Figure 5.1   Channels used by US B2B marketeers to guide leads through the customer journey

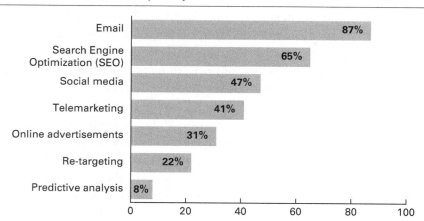

SOURCE 2015 Demand Gen Report Benchmark Study

Many systems also have an intuitive wizard as an option, to design clear and attractive email campaigns or create eye-catching fill-in forms. The import of HTML templates is also generally supported.

More advanced platforms make it possible to dynamize the content of your emails. The system compares the profile of your contact with the range of available content and selects the options that are most suitable for the profile in question. Top-of-the-range systems even offer so-called 'A/B-testing' (also known as 'split testing'). This allocates a variant of the same message to two different test groups. The response results of the two groups are compared, with the more effective of the two variants being used for the mailing to the remaining large majority of your contacts.

An even more sophisticated option – usually as an extra – is the personalization of the sender details: the 'from' field. Depending on the market in which you operate, it is becoming more and more customary to send emails with the name of a specific sender; for example, the name of a seller the contact is used to dealing with. This gives your mail campaign a little additional style.

Dynamic communication

With the range of customer information at your disposal, you can automatically and individually streamline your communication and make it more dynamic. Dynamic content means that what the customer gets to see in your mail has been selected to match their profile information. These adjustments can include the use of specific colours, texts and pop-ups, as well as the composition of the texts. Dynamic forms are forms that ask no more questions than are absolutely necessary. The system already has a lot of information and only requests the additional data that it still needs.

Dynamic pricing is the setting of prices to reflect the profile of your site visitors. A contact who visits your site on several occasions in a relatively short period will be shown a different price to someone who is only visiting the site for the first time. This concept is used, for example, on sites where you can book airline tickets or holidays. However, it can also be useful in certain B2B applications, where it is possible to show an adjusted price to customers belonging to a certain category or a particular discount group.

Providing dynamic personalized content of this kind is, of course, only possible if your system divides up your contacts into different segments. This segmentation is also automated, based on the online behaviour of the contact. Sometimes there is an option to take account of secondary criteria, such as transactional data relating to payment behaviour, the contact's available hardware and software (web browser, operating system, etc) or geographical location.

A summary of content management functionalities:

- lead nurturing;
- lead generation;
- lead scoring;
- customer engagement index;
- real time content personalization;
- sales intelligence;
- inbound marketing;
- customer lifecycle management;
- big data marketing;
- analytics and transaction automation;
- multi-channel marketing;
- dynamic one-on-one emails;

- anonymous marketing automation;

- predictive marketing;

- marketing automation for small online shops;

- integration with CRM, ERP and call centres.

SOURCE SALESManago 2015

CRM and contact management

Marketing automation is possible without CRM. But if you already have a separate contact management or CRM system, it is important that the information detected by marketing automation can be seamlessly matched with the existing system. In this way, the combined information can be shared at all levels of the company. This is essential for the efficiency and effectiveness of your commercial organization.

Marketing automation makes it easier to manage contacts, divide them up into groups, and allocate those groups to particular sales staff. The system also compiles and monitors the customer profiles based on the automatic processing of the traceable information generated by the customers online. Different accounts can also be made for different function profiles within the organization. This will determine, for example, who gets to see what information about which customer and also who is authorized to amend customer profiles.

Advanced marketing automation platforms allow the user to add notes and an individual task list to customer contact cards. This makes it possible for each user of the system to create his or her own personalized CRM work environment. These advanced systems can also be linked to the individual email accounts of the sales team. In this way, the mails that are sent and received via sales are immediately absorbed into the monitoring and automation process, thereby creating a fully integrated email environment.

Lead scoring and nurturing

By now, you might be thinking: 'What's so special about sending an email or two? I could do that! Customer segmentation? You can do that manually as well, can't you? All you need is a pen and a note book! Why should I buy an expensive system for something I can easily do myself? And it's the same with contact management and customer profiling: a little common sense, an Excel spreadsheet and a bit of help from the CRM (if its up-to-date!) and away you go. Tailor-made customer content? Back to my pen and notebook, or maybe a word processor...'

This is all very true, of course, and the choice is up to you. But you need to bear in mind that there are some very specific functionalities that you can only exploit through marketing automation.

> There are some very specific functionalities that you can only exploit through marketing automation.

In selling anything, you will not succeed unless you generate interest amongst your prospects and customers. Marketing automation registers every visitor to your website and investigates the commercial potential of each contact, so that it can signal possible new leads. Even though many of these contacts will quickly fall by the wayside – 85 per cent of your visitors are just exploring possibilities – the system monitors them all: what information they requested, who requested it, how long they stayed on each page, etc.

This information is used to give each contact a score. Prospects are repeatedly ranked on the basis of their changing scores. Lists of the most promising prospects are generated as often as you like. Reaching a certain score may trigger a related action; for example, which communication is sent, how frequently and by whom.

Lead scoring is an essential concept in marketing automation. It allows you to award or deduct points in function of the specific recorded actions taken by your contact. This results in a numerical assessment of the 'relationship-willingness' of each potential customer. Some systems offer more sophisticated scoring methods, positioning the customer relationship in quadrant models and showing the results in heat diagrams. Lead scoring is also often combined with demographic and online behaviour data.

In general, lead scoring can be divided into two different levels: the engagement level (implicit lead scoring) and the fit (explicit lead scoring). The profile of the lead, based on their online behaviour (for example, requesting a white paper), number of clicks and length of stay, is reflected in the engagement level. The extent to which the contact is a good match for your target profile (the type of new customer you hope to attract) is reflected in the fit.

In the better marketing automation packages, the engagement score and the fit are both calculated automatically using algorithms. Sometimes both levels can be visually represented as a certain position within a quadrant matrix. The leads most worth following up are (self-evidently) those with the best possible engagement score in combination with the best possible fit.

The second added value of marketing automation is lead nurturing. This is currently a hot issue. The *2015 Demand Gen Report Benchmark Study* indicated that almost two-thirds of the respondents wanted to test or roll out lead nurturing technology in 2015.[3] The quality of leads is becoming increasingly important, and the latest technology now makes it possible to focus effort and resources where they have most chance of success.

The better marketing automation platforms contain automatic programmes that provide sales teams with a list of sale-ready contacts. These are contacts who have already travelled so far in their customer journey that they have reached the point of final decision-making. This means, of course, that it is no longer necessary to manually assess leads, which in the modern era has become a near impossible task, in view of the speed and frequency with which potential customers now ask for new information. An option with some systems is automated contact routing and the allocation of the process best used to follow up promising leads.

If you want to provide customers with individual service, it is useful if the content you offer them is packaged in a format that is most likely to appeal to them, since this increases the chances of it being read and/or used. The tracking information generated by your marketing automation will tell you, for example, whether a customer is more likely to respond to an email or to suggestions on your website. Some automated systems even have tools that can prepare made-to-measure content, such as HubSpot's Content Generator. In other cases, you may need to buy separate content preparation software, in which you can store various ideas and transform them into blog-ready text.

Automatic content generation

The automatic generation of content is still in its infancy, as the English text reproduced below clearly shows. This text was the result of an experiment conducted by *The Guardian* on the subject of quinoa. It was sent to me by the HubSpot team when I asked them how far they had progressed in their attempt to generate blogs automatically on the basis of the content contained within their automated systems.

'The crime-ridden family of quinoa has taken US by storm this month. According to Peru, New York has confirmed that quinoa is more story than anything else they've ever seen. Quotes from top Yotam Ottolenghi eaters suggest that crop is currently clear top, possibly more than ground black pepper. Experts say both Salt and University need to traditionally grow to strengthen a common solution. Finally, it is worth slightly rattling that this article was peeled until it made sense.'

Amusing though this is, it is expected that the quality of automatically generated contact will improve rapidly in the years ahead before too long, a few mouse clicks will be enough to prepare your blogs and mailings. Some fine-tuning of the texts may be necessary, but the basic structure will be correct and will reflect current best practice relating to findability, native content matching, legibility and shareability.

Drip marketing and alerts

Marketing automation also makes it possible for you to set up drip campaigns that can be automatically triggered. Drip marketing, as the name implies, means that you communicate your message to the (potential) customer drip by drip, gradually building up interest. You only do this with contacts who meet pre-set criteria or after they have demonstrated pre-set behaviour online. If your contact has downloaded a folder about one of your products, your next step might be to send them more detailed information or perhaps even to make a proposal.

Drip campaigns are usually carried out via email, but can also be extended to include social media. The content of each communication is specifically geared to the interests and needs indicated by the target contact's actions. Your automatic system will be aware of these interests (monitored in real time). It will therefore know which message needs to be sent at which time to move the contact further along the sales funnel in the direction of a purchase.

A further functionality that CRM and marketing automation systems have in common is the automatic generation and allocation of tasks and the automatic issuing of warning signals or alerts when urgent action needs to be taken. For example, some systems automatically dispatch notifications to relevant staff whenever a (potential) customer performs a certain action online. This might, for example, be a message to sales recommending that the moment has come to make contact with the prospect.

In a similar way, automatic task lists can remind you of things that need to be done. Perhaps the moment has come to post a new webinar on social media for your current email campaign. Or maybe the time is ripe to start your email canvassing for the forthcoming congress.

Last but not least, a wide range of other actions can be automated. This simply depends on how you programme your marketing system. A wide range of specific behaviours on the part of the prospect or customer can be linked to an equally wide range of pre-defined automatic responses, adjusted to reflect the contact's specific profile. In this way, you can continue to add value at all stages of the customer journey.

Analysis and reporting

In addition to the opportunity to scale up highly efficient personalized marketing campaigns for the requirements of larger groups of (potential) customers, marketing automation yields yet another significant advantage. It provides you with the tools to analyse in depth the online behaviour of (potential) customers and their reaction to your opening value proposition, collating the findings in a series of clear reports and key figures.

The most common online tools are those that measure the online activity of contacts. This tells you what content scores well and which messages are the most successful. Other standard tools can measure the performance of your landing page, the content that you offer online, the mails you send and the campaigns you implement. These tools also trace the sources of your web traffic.

More advanced marketing automation platforms have additional functionalities, such as the optimization of your content for search engines. SEO keyword analytics allows you to see how your content is currently ranked for search in Google, Yahoo!, etc.

The very best platforms measure ROI per campaign and monitor the level of invested capital against the number of prospects and the amount of additional return generated. The system registers and cross-references all relevant data. If a customer buys something, the system logs it in their online history.

It is also possible to print off reports about the success ratio of separate sales teams and separate actions, as well as the effect that these actions have on the contacts in question. Some systems even go so far as to quantify the costs that need to be incurred to move a lead through each phase of the sales process.

CASE STUDY

Predictive intelligence

Predictive intelligence is a method of delivering experiences tuned specifically to the unique context of each individual. Nothing strange, you could argue, since you're already personalizing content, services and products to the preferences gathered in your customers' profiles. Except, these profiles are built on historical behaviour or information the customer was willing to share in the past.

Predictive intelligence on the other hand uses algorithms to enhance the customer's profile in realtime, using information it gathers in real time through live customer behaviour at that moment. This living profile is then used to supply content or ship products automatically, based on predicted estimates of the actions a customer might take or the things they might be interested in. This content is delivered through to the web, mobile or email and even a call centre.

According to SalesForce, predictive intelligence lifts website revenue by 10 per cent, email click through rates by 35 per cent, and email conversion rates by 25 per cent.[4]

> 'Predictive intelligence enhance the customer's profile in real time, capitalizing on actual customer behavior at that moment.'

Predictive intelligence is already everywhere. Purchase an electric guitar from an online music shop and you will receive automatic suggestions to consider accessories like specific sound effect pedals. Not just some random sound effect, but a sound effect which makes a perfect twin with the guitar you bought, in addition to your past purchasing behaviour and that of similar customers.

Or, suppose you're working on a project for a few days in a row on-site at a client's office. You return home late in the evening, but not before getting some food nearby. Over the past few days, you have repeatedly searched online for a restaurant close to that location and at approximately the same time, also stating your preference for Italian food over Chinese, or vice versa.

Predictive intelligence will detect the pattern and perhaps suggest a new place with excellent ratings, or a special menu at the usual place. The algorithm might even have detected that the meal is more pragmatic than romantic, based on the amount of time you spend at the restaurant, suggesting a convenient place close to the motorway.

Predictive analysis is all about the convenience game. A standard and repetitive shopping list becomes an algorithm, and someone else takes over the responsibility of filling your fridge. When Amazon carries out anticipatory shipping, it offers the convenience of you knowing that you'll never run out of toilet paper.[5] The internet of things can be used for data collection and in turn, for gathering insights on customer behaviour.

App tracking and beacons

Marketing automation is also gradually moving into the world of apps and mobile devices. Companies like SALESManago are setting the pace with their experiments in app tracking and the integration of beacons into marketing automation.

App tracking brings automated marketing right to the very heart of your smartphone: its ultra-informative range of installed apps. App tracking makes it possible to apply a number of marketing automation functions to app use. One of the most recent (which I only recently saw demonstrated) was the ability to identify which apps a person has downloaded onto their phone. 'Show me your apps and I will tell you who you are.' The possibilities are endless!

Beacons and near-field communication devices are Bluetooth trackers and transmitters that make it feasible to actually enter into dialogue with customers and to provide them with information direct to their smartphone. This involves both the detection of the smartphone (beacon) and the reception of signals (near-field) when the customer comes somewhere in the vicinity of a transmitter. This technology has numerous potential applications in the retail sector, but also at trade fairs and in offices. In this way, it is possible to register customer interests in the real world in real time.

Near-field communication likewise opens the door to numerous possibilities at points of sale. In particular, it provides the opportunity to link displays to the customer's digital journey and (of course!) to record these in the customer touchpoint mapping function. The trajectory followed by a contact in a shop or at a trade fair provides useful information.

In a similar manner, VR – virtual reality – will soon become standard. As a result, the visual reception and absorption of information, the lifelike simulation of the use of a product or service and the replacement of classic demos with VR experiences will soon become the rule rather than the exception.

Moreover, the combination of the internet of things and Industry 4.0 with the increasing use of drones will develop new possibilities, of which entrepreneurs until now have only been able to dream!

For one of our customers – Group Suerickx, a default disruptive company that is quickly gaining ground in the industrial and residential renovation market – we recently developed a brand-new CRM system. One of its features is that the completion of an enquiry form by a lead is immediately and automatically linked to a top view and a street view via Google. These two images appear alongside the address in the CRM profile of the lead.

This makes it possible for everyone inside the company involved in the project to inspect the roof and gable of the property, without the need to actually visit it. As a consequence, company personnel are able to ask relevant questions of interest to the potential customer.

Nowadays, more and more experiments are taking place for the delivery of packages by drone. It is not unthinkable that in the near future companies will consider buying into the camera images and recording opportunities that these drones make possible, if they happen to pass over the location of one of your target contacts. This would mean that without the need to have a drone of your own, you could fully map the on-site situation of any building or piece of ground.

It sounds like one of those detective films, where video images from security and traffic cameras are used to track the criminal, but it could very soon become commercial reality. It may even become feasible to integrate drone images in your GoToMeeting, so that you can exchange thoughts with your customer while analysing the problem in real time from a height of 120 metres!

CASE STUDY

Amazon Prime Air is Amazon's next delivery option

The book which Amazon ships to your home address without you having ordered it, anticipating your future reading habits and by that way also steering these habits, may well be delivered by air. Amazon Prime Air is a delivery system from Amazon designed to safely get packages to customers in 30 minutes or less using drones. In 2016 they were already flying up to 20 miles at speeds faster than 50 mph.[6]

Amazon is testing many different unmanned drone configurations and delivery mechanisms in a variety of operation environments, particularly in development centres such as the United States, United Kingdom, Austria, France and Israel. The drones deliver packages weighing less than five pounds and this possible payload covers 86 per cent of the packages Amazon ships today.[7] The first Amazon drone delivery to an actual customer took place on December 7, 2016 in the Cambridge area of England.[8] Then on March 17 a few months later, a drone delivered a box of sunscreen at an Amazon-hosted conference in Palms Springs, US.[9]

Although still in a test phase and with regulations that need amendment first (likely to take a while) Amazon says that one day, seeing Prime Air vehicles will be as normal as seeing mail trucks on the road.[10] It is set to make Prime Air just one of the possible delivery options.[11]

With a 30-minute delivery window, in most cases Amazon will beat travel time to a shop. Not only will the customer be notified when the drone and package set off, the app will also count down the minutes and seconds of airtime to delivery. The one thing you'll need on the receiving end of the drone delivery is the Amazon-branded landing mat you can print out at home, acting as a home beacon for the drone.[12]

With a 30-minute delivery window, in most cases Amazon will beat travel time to a shop.

CASE STUDY

How UPS is working on a hybrid truck–drone delivery system

Drone technology seems to change logistics configurations altogether. One of the limitations in drone delivery is the distance radius of the drone itself. Innovation combining existing and new technologies is pushing boundaries rapidly forward, increasing drone usefulness.

UPS for example tested a combined package truck and drone delivery system, where the truck also acts as a mobile local delivery hub.[13] It consists of a new type of electric delivery truck with a drone dock, plus a launch pad on top of it. A cage suspended beneath the drone extends through a hatch into the truck. A UPS driver inside loads a package into the cage and presses a button on a touch screen, sending the drone on a pre-set route to an address.

The drone then flies autonomously to its destination, leaving the driver free to make other deliveries on the route. After the package is released, the drone autonomously returns to the package car at a planned stop and autonomously redocks. The battery-powered drone recharges while it's docked. The battery enables the drone to make 30-minute flights and the maximum deadweight of the drone is 10 lbs.

> Innovation combining existing and new technologies is pushing boundaries rapidly forward, increasing drone usefulness.

The hybrid truck–drone delivery system promises important time and cost gains, especially in rural areas where delivery stops are miles apart, or in triangularly spread out routes. Sending a drone from a package car to make just one of those deliveries can significantly reduce miles driven and help drivers to save time and deliver on increasing customer service needs that stem from the growth of ecommerce.

UPS has been testing automation and robotics technologies, including drones, for years. In September 2016, a UPS drone delivered an asthma inhaler from Beverly, Mass, to a youth camp on an island three miles off the Atlantic coast.

Additionally, UPS is using drones extensively for humanitarian relief, partnering with third-party organizations to deliver life-saving healthcare products like blood and vaccines to hard-to-reach locations. The first flights of medical supplies were conducted in October 2016 in Rwanda. UPS is also utilizing drones to confirm stock or available space on high storage shelves in its warehouses in Louisville, Kentucky and Venlo, Netherlands.[14]

In the future, UPS will extend test cases to increase operational efficiency to include inventory management, facility monitoring and external equipment inspection. However, the hybrid truck–drone delivery system shows how drones might assist in making non-urgent residential deliveries as part of day-to-day operations.

Something for everyone

It is no longer a matter of price. Applications that were once only within the budget of large companies are now affordable for SMEs.

> Applications that were once only within the budget of large companies are now affordable for SMEs.

You can now lease a really good marketing automation package from as little as €299 per month. If you want something more advanced, it will probably cost you €600 per month. If you want real state-of-the-art, we are probably talking somewhere between €1,500 and €3,500 per month. But even for just €299, you will be able to find out who is visiting your website and who is reading your mails, as well as collecting profile information about your prospects, sending targeted mailings, allocating tasks and, ultimately, deciding when the prospect is sale-ready.

You can even find something cheaper if you are really strapped for cash, but these packages only offer small-player solutions, often still in beta. Even so, this can sometimes be sufficient for some customers and some pilots. You pay your money and you make your choice.

In some ways, it is a disadvantage (or is it an advantage?) that there are so many marketing tools on the market. The majority of them offer more or less the same functional options, but they each have their own special features and differences. This doesn't make it easy to find the best one for you. So what criteria should you use to make your choice?

Technology for the marketer

In his Chief Marketing Technologist blog, Scott Brinker, the chief technology officer of I-on Interactive, gives regular summaries of the available marketing technology. The summaries list all the tools available today that companies could ever need to shape customer experience, manage operations, process data, automate marketing, work in the cloud, organize social media marketing, set up ecommerce, etc, etc.

Brinker's blog looks like a tufted logo carpet! But the strength and depth of the summary proves beyond question just how closely marketing and technology have become intertwined in recent years and how modern marketing has moved far beyond the stage of simply organizing adverts and promo campaigns.

The main difficulty for today's marketeers is to navigate their way through this technological maze and to find the time to learn and use their chosen tools in a focused and integrated manner. But this is just the start: according to Brinker the next big difficulty will be that many of the technology providers will increasingly work together or even merge. Consolidation (and all that it implies) is inevitable.

Brinker's technology map is too detailed to reproduce in this book, but you can view it by scanning the QR code below. Managers will find this a useful exercise to check what technology their marketing people nowadays have at their disposal.

Figure 5.2   QR code: Scott Brinker's technology map

Choosing from 5,381 marketing technology solutions

Year after year, the overview map of marketing technology applications composed by Scott Brinker gains in sheer volume. With thousands of logos cropped into the self-defined 'super-graphic', his technology poster is almost a form of modern art, generating both enthusiasm and – quite understandably – feelings of utter panic.

Compared to 2016, the marketing technology landscape that Brinker presented in May 2017 at the MarTech conference in San Francisco, grew again by about 40 per cent, reaching *5,381 solutions* in total. These are made up of 4,891 unique companies, an increase of 40 per cent from 2016.

Solutions are devised into six category groups:

- advertising and promotion;
- content and experience;
- social and relationships;
- commerce and sales;
- data;
- management.

The growth in both numbers and the diversity of solutions available is quite fascinating and illustrates the change and digitization in marketing and sales. A few years ago, in 2011, Brinker only mapped 150 solutions.

The growth in both numbers and diversity of marketing technology solutions illustrates the change and digitization in marketing and sales.

Last year, Brinker detected (as he calls it) 'a non-trivial amount of churn', as 4.7 per cent of the solutions from 2016 were removed and another 3.5 per cent were renamed or refocused. However, the exit rate of companies and solutions was widely exceeded by the new additions and entrants.

What is interesting, says Brinker, is the long tail distribution of marketing technology vendors, with a few massive blockbusters, thousands of smaller and micro Software as a Service-companies (SaaS), plus niche innovators. In contrast with other digital platform technology markets, the major players did not downplay the blossoming ecosystem.

In 2017, Brinker stated: 'The spectacular scope explosion of marketing – and the rate at which new disruptions and innovations continue to rule marketing and business at large – has made it impossible for any vendor to deliver everything that a marketer needs in a digital world... Almost all of the major providers now acknowledge this, and they've shifted their strategies to embrace the ecosystem – becoming true "platforms" that make it easier for marketers to plug in a variety of more specialized and vertical solutions.'[15]

Most of the bigger Martech platforms and cloud-based solutions are designed as centralized hubs where other solutions can plug into, just like a wheel with its central hub and spokes. However, Brinker also depicts a far more distributed and organic approach, ignoring the plan of a centralized hub architecture, mimicking the more social organizational models and building on a commons of data.

'On the other end of the spectrum from centralized platforms, integration-Platform-as-a-Service (iPaaS) solutions let companies create "distributed" platforms — dynamically piping data between marketing applications and their own independent marketing data lakes',[16] he says.

This organic architecture offers the benefit of its adaptability to change. Yet another group of platforms emerges, says Brinker, blending both worlds in a hybrid fashion, combining both centralized and distributed platform designs; a blend between centralized and distributed philosophies. Examples are data management platforms, customer data platforms and real-time interaction management.

More than ever, it seems that form follows function. 'Instead of choosing suite or best-of-breed, many marketers are now combining these two approaches — using the suites as digital marketing hubs and then augmenting them with a range of more specialized products to bake their own, special marketing and customer experience cake,' Brinker states.[17]

Ignoring the plan of a centralized hub architecture, and mimicking the more social organizational models is the way an increasing number of companies choose to operate.

Brinker offers keen permission to reproduce copies of his 'Martech 5,000' super-graphic in any media, as long as it is reproduced in full. Personally, I like to do so, since it strengthens the overall message I'm trying to sell. The result is quite teasing, but also a bit out of place.

Figure 5.3   The Marketing Technology Landscape ('Martech 5,000')

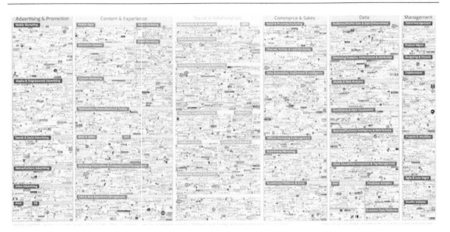

Source   chiefmartec.com, May 2017

Don't worry, you don't need glasses! A readable version of the super-graphic would need at least an origami-like folded coffee table sized book, and even then, the logos would be difficult to decipher for the unenhanced eye.

In fact, the pixelated illustration shown here is only included to tease you, deliberately stressing the fact that although technology is there with the purpose to make our life easier and drive growth and success in general, the sheer abundance of solutions also generates wild complexity and an overwhelming feeling of not seeing the wood for the trees. Convince yourself there is more out there than you knew and know and download the full-scale hi-res version of the Martech 5,000 from chiefmartec.com.

But at the same time, more specialist parties will rise on top of what already exists, in whatever format. It's a bit like a new era in Martech life, where tech's nature took its next step in a changing environment, making it possible for a new kind of tech breeds to live and prosper.

At CPI, we advise many companies on composing the ideal tech stack. We are confronted with the impact and the complexity of the marketing technology landscape on a daily basis.

Figure 5.4   QR code: The Martech 5,000 on chiefmartec.com

We continue to have very good experiences with the use of SalesForce, which has evolved from a CRM platform into a full ecosystem. This allows a variety of functions to operate in a dynamic way. In many companies we are seeing a trend towards moving away from all encompassing ERP and a move towards architectures using a thin layer of ERP, such as SAP for key processes (finance, purchasing and production planning); plus a layer of other more flexible functions organized in the CRM. For other projects we use iSaaS (integrated Services as a Solution) to connect different platforms and tools – completely in line with Scott Brinker's vision on working with distributed solutions.

Taking into account the rapid evolution of technology and the emerging importance of new concepts such as speech to text, semantic analysis and the internet of things, it has to be accepted that tech stacks cannot be built for eternity but require regular reviews and updates every six months. This is to catch up with evolving user requirements and any new possibilities on offer for better efficiency or customer orientation.

> Taking into account the rapid evolution of technology, it has to be accepted that marketing tech stacks cannot be built for eternity but require regular reviews and updates.

The end of talking, the rise of texting

> Of those aged between 18–24 who are given a choice between only being able to text or only being able to call, around 75 per cent chose texting.

One of the major developments for 2017 is the proliferation of the chatbot. This revolution follows another trend, in which people younger than 24 show a tendency to prefer texting over speaking. Already in 2013, a UK study[18] discovered schoolchildren as young as eight with a growing proficiency in bilingualism. Contrary to your expectations, this second language is textspeak.

Two out of three teachers said they regularly find textspeak like IMO (in my opinion), YOYO (you are on your own), THX (thank you) or ATM (at the moment) in their pupils' homework. Over the past five years, texting and online messaging have exploded in popularity, becoming a preferred communication tool for young people.

The number of monthly texts being sent over the net increased more than 7,700 per cent over the last decade[19]. Of those aged between 18–24 and given a choice between only being able to text or only being able to call, around 75 per cent chose texting. Also, 75 per cent of millennials preferred to receive texts for things like appointments, payments, order alerts, and so on.[20]

> People younger than 24 show a preference for texting over speaking. This has a major impact on how companies should organize customer interaction in the near future.

The tendency to adopt text to speech is influenced by the context of our modern life, in which time is scarce and the ability to multitask and handle different tasks at the same time has become a standard expectation. Most jobs require employees to balance competing demands for their time and energy, and employers expect you to be able to handle multiple priorities. Even at home, our attention is divided between different screens. While watching TV, we are liking and sharing social media posts and chatting with our friends via tablets and smartphones.

---

10 reasons why millennials don't answer your phone calls anymore[21]

1 phone calls are disruptive;

2 phone calls are presumptuous;

3 phone calls are time consuming;

4 phone calls are inefficient;

5 phone calls are annoying;

6 phone calls are stressful;

7 phone calls are superfluous;

8 phone calls aren't private;

9 phone calls aren't personal;

10 phone calls aren't on my time

'No chat, no conversation.' This is what we try to explain to our clients when they are hesitating to engage in the use of a chat function or a chatbot on their website and in their engagement portals. You can read more on this below.

Another advantage of the texting era: it makes the analysis of conversations easier. In the case of speech, you first had to transcribe the spoken work into text, a time-consuming process before you could even think about analysing the content.

When texting is the medium, all of the information that needs to be analysed is readily available. This allows us to conduct projects which identify the 'language of the customer' or to run analytics on positive and negative trends, key words used in conversations and trending topics, all in a very efficient and affordable way.

Live Chat is nearly as popular as phone and email

When you have a question or problem you need help with, how do you like to connect with a company's customer service group?

Based on 1,426 consumers in the US, UK, Ireland, Mexico and Columbia:[22]

- phone conversation with a live person: 58%;
- email: 54%;
- live chat: 48%;
- text message: 17%;
- phone conversation with an interactive voice recognition system: 17%.

According to the 2016 Aspect Consumer Experience Index, 49 per cent of US consumers aged 18-65 would prefer their customer service interactions via text, chat or messaging[23] and 39 per cent of consumers find texting a more effective communication tool then talking when engaging with a company.[24] Assuming the quality of the experience and privacy are assured, 40 per cent really like the idea customer service via messaging apps (like Facebook Messenger, WhatsApp, Slack, Snapchat and so on).

The interest and demand for automated and self-service experiences continues to rise: 69 per cent of consumers in the study say they interact with an intelligent assistant or chatbot at least once a month (making the assumption that people are able to distinguish a human chat from a botchat); and 71 per cent of consumers want the ability to solve most customer service issues on their own, up from 64 per cent in 2015.[25]

Consumers who have not used chatbots have a critical stance towards the experience as a whole. However, once they have experienced a chatbot interaction, customers rate their experience higher than expected.

How to make your choice

The basic questions

Every successful implementation begins with the careful and accurate mapping out of what your organization wants to achieve with automation technology. It is easiest to do this by charting a customer journey, detailing what role you expect technology and automation to play during each phase and how this role can be linked to your commercial objectives.

Decide what functionalities you need

The following summary lists the marketing automation functions that are currently most popular in the marketplace. This means that these are the tools your competitors will soon be using – if they aren't already.

This list was compiled by Demand Gen, an American world player in marketing automation. Demand Gen asked B2B marketeers which (combination of) marketing tools they most wanted to test or roll out in 2015.

Search for possible suppliers

Check online your desired functions one by one against the specifications provided by potential suppliers. Based on what you find, you will gradually refine your own selection criteria, since you will probably discover new information – and new applications – of which you were not originally aware.

At this stage, price is also another important factor that needs to be taken into consideration, as is the feasibility of integrating the proposed solution into your existing systems architecture and linking it with current data sources.

Figure 5.5   Which marketing automation tools were wanted to test or roll out in 2015?

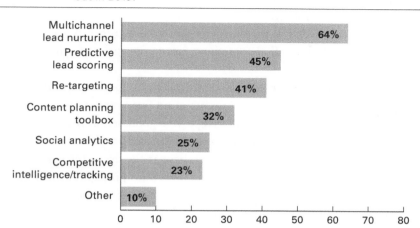

SOURCE 2015 Demand Gen Report Benchmark Study

Make a selection and carry out thorough testing

Most suppliers of marketing automation technology allow their applications to be tested in practice for a reasonable period of time, usually 30 days. These test drives are extremely useful. But bear in mind that a test project of this kind also costs your company time and money – so make sure that it is clearly defined and approached seriously. You don't want to have to go cap in hand to your customers to explain that a particular action is no longer available because you have changed your software provider!

Also remember that 30 days is not really long enough to fully test and evaluate the worth of a system as complex as marketing automation. You should therefore view your test more as something to confirm your decision rather than make your decision.

At CPI we work with a number of different marketing automation packages that we use for our customers. We have a basic version (cheap and limited), a mid-range version (robust and sufficient for most companies) and two top-of-the-range versions. The latter can do just about anything, one for content marketing and the other for ecommerce.

We use these packages to set up pilot projects for a period of three to six months, working to specific target groups with fully developed campaigns (mailings, socials, re-marketing, lead scoring, integration with sales and customer service, etc). This longer period makes it possible to see what is important and what is irrelevant; what works and what still needs further fine-tuning. And all without the customer needing to invest a penny in their own marketing technology.

If the trial is successful, the customer can continue to lease our system, or else we will help them find something more appropriate to their specific circumstances.

If you want to conduct your own search for a marketing automation system, the procedure outlined below is a good but simple test to check the functionalities you require. It will give you a good sense of the extent to which the system is likely to live up to your expectations. You can set up the test internally, using your own team members as the users. Or perhaps you can enlist the help of loyal customers in a mini-pilot project that will (hopefully) convince you both of the benefits of this kind of technology.

Perform the following actions to assess each system:

- install a tracking code on your site;
- create a new email account (including graphics and buttons);
- import a contact data set;
- make a new landing page (including graphics and call to actions);
- send a simple mail marketing campaign to a test group within the company;
- arrange a drip action for the test subjects with an email, a re-targeting action and an SMS;
- analyse the interaction report and check if the standard parameters provide you with useful information;
- assess precisely what information is stored in the system, how easily you can add new information to it and how you can transfer this information to your CRM system;
- evaluate the extent to which the system provides benefits for your customers in terms of proactivity, access to information and better customer care.

Closing the deal

A last important item is, of course, the conditions of the contract; more particularly, the price and how to pay. There are many different types of contract. How flexible is yours? Can it easily be amended or terminated? What if the number of users increases significantly? Also check to make sure there are no hidden costs in the form of extras outside the basic contract.

Some suppliers charge different prices depending on the number of active contacts you have. If your database contains 500,000 names and addresses, you will pay considerably more than if it only contains 5,000. But for some other packages there is no relationship between your number of contacts and the monthly price, which means that you will always know in advance what you need to pay each month. Sometimes the price is dependent on the number of work stations on which the system operates.

The place of marketing technology in your organization

Every marketing department worth the name nowadays needs to be staffed with people who have a tried and tested in-depth knowledge of marketing technology. You can either appoint a CMTO – Chief Marketing Technology Officer – within the unit, or else you can outsource the task. But what place will this marketing technology occupy within your marketing organization?

Chief Marketing Technologist Scott Brinker believes that strategy and creativity still take precedence over marketing technology.[26] The technology itself cannot provide the leadership, strategy and creativity that lead to success. Technology can certainly inspire and make possible the implementation of brilliant ideas. And good marketing technology will continually open up new possibilities for the strategists and the innovators. However, technological wizardry alone can never make good a lack of inventiveness or an absence of clear guidance at company level.

However, as soon as the technology is brought into line with the strategic and creative thinking of the company, the technological imperatives must be given precedence over other operational and tactical considerations. A large part of the strength of marketing technology rests in its ability to efficiently automate, optimize and accelerate marketing processes. This frees up resources and people to be used elsewhere, where they can make a more telling contribution to the overall company objectives.

The added value of marketing technology

Here are 20 ways in which marketing technology can add value for your organisation:

1 Visitors to your website will be identified. Marketing automation will check their behaviour. You can define the importance of each customer with automatic criteria.

Figure 5.6   The sweet spot of marketing technology in the organization

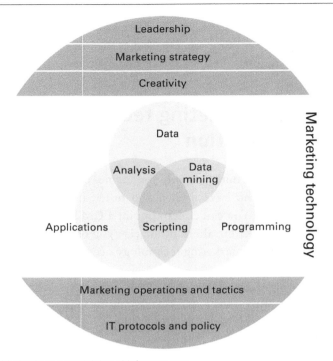

Leadership

Marketing strategy

Creativity

Data

Analysis   Data mining

Applications   Scripting   Programming

Marketing operations and tactics

IT protocols and policy

Marketing technology

SOURCE With thanks to Scott Brinker, chiefmartec.com

2 You can monitor the behavioural activity of the visitor on sub-pages and identify the elements that are important to them. Analysis of scroll and click activity will make it possible to evaluate which products and elements are most interesting for the customer, even if they fail to click on further sub-pages.

3 Marketing technology highlights the interests of every company that visits your website. This gives valuable insights to your sales team, allowing them to make proposals based on the specific interests of specific companies.

4 You can build up an extensive knowledge about customers without ever meeting them. Everyone in the company can have access to their profiles, without ever needing to leave their work post.

5 You can compile tailor-made (weekly) newsletters. The contents, with messages and/or proposals, are automatically personalized on the basis of the interests shown by your contacts. The sending is also automatic, based on a previously programmed protocol.

6   The system not only shows you the best day but also the best time of day to send an offer to particular contacts, based on their past reading history. This function allows the full automation of offer dispatch.

7   Emails sent to (potential) customers are automatically monitored. Every seller knows when the (potential) customer opens a mail and/or clicks on a proposal, as well as if or when they return to your website and what products and services they view.

8   After a contact has visited your website, you can automatically send follow-up mails with personalized messages at the time most likely to attract their attention. The content of the message is automatically adjusted to reflect the interests they have shown on the website.

9   The dynamic content of the website can be automatically adjusted to suit each individual visitor. Different banners can be selected for both potential customers and actual customers.

10 The system gives potential customers a lead score. This allows salesmen to focus their attention on the most promising prospects.

11 Potential customers are automatically divided into segments on the basis on their online behaviour and past transaction details.

12 The system automatically generates both the sales funnel and the market-ing campaigns that will lead contacts through the different phases of the customer journey until an effective purchase is made.

13 The landing pages that the visitors see are generated dynamically. Each visitor is offered different made-to-measure content, depending on their demographic, contact, behaviour and transaction details.

14 The profile of every visitor is automatically and progressively updated. This happens via dynamic contact forms, which only request informa-tion not previously known.

15 Re-targeting technology allows you to reach visitors who viewed your website anonymously, using adverts on the site and social media.

16 You can continuously monitor the behaviour of customers throughout the sales cycle. When the customer's movement through the sales funnel slows down, the sales department is automatically alerted, so that auto-matic mails can be sent to encourage further progress.

17 Leads are automatically assessed and approached. For example, lead routing with selected buttons, distribution to local sale offices, the type of product, the origin of the customer and so on.

18 You can automatically send cyclical mails – for example, a promotional offer for a new product that the visitor viewed on your website when it was launched onto the market. This increases the likelihood of a sale.

19 Refresher mails can automatically be sent to contacts who have not visited your website for some time, in the hope of enticing them back for a new visit.

20 The sales department or call centre is automatically alerted when a live contact with a customer is recommended and when the customer in question is online.

Notes

1 SALESManago [accessed Dec 2017] Marketing Automation – The Definitive and Ultimate Guide to Marketing Automation [Online] https://www.salesmanago.com/info/definitve_and_ultimate_new_knowledge.htm

2 SALESManago [accessed Dec 2017]

3 Demand Gen [accessed June 2015] 2015 Demand Gen Report Benchmark Study – What's Working In Demand Generation [Online] http://www.demandgenreport.com/industry-resources/research/3090-2015-benchmark-study-whats-working-in-demand-generation.html

4 Hutchinson, Matthew [accessed May 2017] What is Predictive Intelligence – and Why Should Every Marketer Care?, *Salesforce* [Online] https://www.salesforce.com/blog/2015/08/predictive-intelligence-definition.html

5 Kopalle, Praveen [accessed May 2017] Why Amazon's Anticipatory Shipping Is Pure Genius, *Forbes* [Online] https://www.forbes.com/sites/onmarketing/2014/01/28/why-amazons-anticipatory-shipping-is-pure-genius

6 Nickelsburg, Monica [accessed May 2017] Jeff Bezos: Amazon drones will find landing spots using symbols printed out by customers, *GeekWire* [Online] https://www.geekwire.com/2016/jeff-bezos-amazon-drones-will-find-landing-spots-using-symbols-printed-customers/

7 Nickelsburg [accessed May 2017]

8 Wikipedia [accessed May 2017] Amazon Prime Air [Online] https://en.wikipedia.org/wiki/Amazon_Prime_Air

9 Glaser, April [accessed May 2017] Watch Amazon's Prime Air make its first public US drone delivery, *Recode* [Online] https://www.recode.net/2017/3/24/15054884/amazon-prime-air-public-us-drone-delivery

10 Amazon [accessed May 2017] Amazon Prime Air [Online] https://www.amazon.com/Amazon-Prime-Air/b?node=8037720011

11   Johnson, Luke [accessed May 2017] 9 things you need to know about the Amazon Prime Air drone delivery service, *Digital Spy* [Online] http://www. digitalspy.com/tech/feature/a820748/amazon-prime-air-drone-delivery-service/

12   Johnson [accessed May 2017]

13   UPS [accessed May 2017] UPS Tests Residential Delivery Via Drone Launched From atop Package Car [Online] https://pressroom.ups.com/ pressroom/ContentDetailsViewer.page?ConceptType=PressReleases &id=1487687844847-162

14   UPS [accessed May 2017] Drone Usage Takes Flight at UPS [Online] https:// pressroom.ups.com/mobile0c9a66/assets/pdf/pressroom/infographic/UPS_ drone%20activities_infographic_FINAL.pdf

15   Brinker, Scott [accessed July 2015] Put strategy and creative ahead of marketing technology, *chiefmartec.com* [Online] http://chiefmartec.com/ 2011/05/marketing-technologys-place-in-marketing/

16   Brinker [accessed July 2015]

17   Brinker [accessed July 2015]

18   Merritt, Anne [accessed May 2017] Text-speak: language evolution or just laziness?, *The Telegraph* [Online] http://www.telegraph.co.uk/education/ educationopinion/9966117/Text-speak-language-evolution-or-just-laziness.html

19   Burke, Kenneth [accessed May 2017] 63 Texting Statistics That Answer All Your Questions, *Text Request* [Online] https://www.textrequest.com/blog/ texting-statistics-answer-questions/

20   Lee, Joel [accessed May 2017] These 3 Text Messaging Stats Will Surely Surprise You, *MakeUseOf* [Online] http://www.makeuseof.com/tag/ text-messaging-stats-surprise/

21   Burke, Kenneth [accessed May 2017] 10 Reasons Millennials Aren't Answering Your Phone Calls, *Text Request* [Online] https://www.textrequest. com/blog/10-reasons-millennials-arent-answering-phone-calls/

22   An, Mimi [accessed May 2017] Artificial Intelligence Is Here - People Just Don't Realize It, *HubSpot* [Online] https://research.hubspot.com/reports/ artificial-intelligence-is-here

23   Kim, Larry [accessed May 2017] 10 Fascinating Facts About Chatbots, *LinkedIn* [Online] https://www.linkedin.com/pulse/10-fascinating-facts-chatbots-larry-kim

24   Aspect [accessed May 2017] 2016 Aspect Consumer Experience Index [Online] https://www.aspect.com/globalassets/2016-aspect-consumer- experience-index-survey_index-results-final.pdf

25   Aspect [accessed May 2017]

26   Brinker [accessed July 2015]

Augmented and virtual reality in business

06

> Augmented and virtual reality are becoming more and more important in sales and marketing. The introduction of IOS 11 makes AR and VR functionalities possible on every iPhone.

A new reality?

With the explosion of online selling and customers becoming more and more acquainted with money-saving and time-saving shopping experiences, retailers need to reconsider their role and the value they add in the new convenience-seeking world. For classic retailers, mixing in-store retail with online experiences is not always the easiest answer, since every online business demands its very own business and cost model.

It's all about the customer experience. New visualization techniques like mixed reality make it possible for retailers to blur the line between physical, online and mobile. Mixed reality can pair the ease of online shopping with the thrill of augmented real-life experience,[1] making the retail customer experience more relevant for today's connected consumers.

> **Different forms of reality[2,3,4]**
>
> *Virtual reality* is an artificial environment that is created with software and presented to the user in such a way that the user suspends belief and accepts it as a real environment. On a computer, this physical presence in a virtual or imaginary environment is primarily experienced through two of the five senses: sight and sound.

Augmented reality (AR) is a live direct or indirect view of a physical, real-world environment whose elements are augmented (or supplemented) by computer-generated sensory input such as sound, video, graphics or GPS data. Wikipedia (2017)[5] gives a definition of AR as related to a more general concept called computer-mediated reality, in which a view of reality is modified and possibly even diminished rather than augmented by a computer.

Diminished reality diminishes parts of the physical world by digitally removing unwanted objects from our view. It is the opposite of AR.

Mediated reality alters our perception of reality by adding and removing information through a device such as a headset or smartphone in real time. Mediated reality offers a more informed visual experience, rather than just using AR alone.

Creating customer enchantment across web and mobile channels, in physical stores and in the delivery process becomes the number one challenge for marketeers.

Mixed reality combines the best elements of AR and virtual reality. While virtual reality builds a digital world in all aspects, AR overlays your real world with computer-generated input, in order to enrich the physical space. It modifies a real-world view by overlaying it with other images, sounds and feedback, using 'markers' to determine where the digital elements should be shown.

Combining AR technology with mediated reality lets you identify objects in the real world and attach information to these objects, like technical data, tourist information and possibly even smells. The beautiful thing is, the mix of realities is generated in real time. Still sounds exotic? Think about the Pokémon Go craze.

Currently, virtual reality has its implications for online shopping. Companies are already implementing virtual show rooms where visitors can walk through wearing 3D goggles. One example of its use in retail surroundings can be found at US home improvement chain Lowe's: the Lowe's Holoroom online tool lets customers design their bathroom or kitchen and then explore it in 360° fashion, wearing a 3D mounted headset. Customers can even publish their virtual walk as a YouTube video.[6]

Virtual reality allows online shoppers to decorate empty, virtual rooms to get a feel for products.

Yet it is AR that has the biggest stake in retail, allowing online shoppers to try and compare different products at home, up-front in the choosing-buying-process, without preceding commitments. At the moment, AR has been to be much more impactful in this space than virtual reality, but mixed reality serves both purposes for shoppers in a seamless way: shop through a virtual room, then see how the products you like would look in your own home before deciding whether to purchase them.

As AR becomes part of daily life thanks to the integration in the iPad or the increasing use of Microsoft Hololens in office and workshop environments, we can start living in a multi-level reality, opening up tremendous possibilities for experience delivery, improved communication and knowledge transfer.

Mixed reality technology will become more and more readily available and omnipresent. Every device fitted with a screen and a camera becomes a potential AR-window. In cars, top-notch windscreens already reveal crucial drive information, enhancing safety on the road. You can already try out a different hairstyle on your mobile before even making an appointment with the hairdresser or make a bear dance on the palm of your hand. A simple advert in a magazine becomes an in-house display and product simulator. A printed article becomes a video screen. Focus your camera on a hotel and you can browse for room availability and even look inside the rooms and make a booking.[7]

Consumer interest in using AR will only grow over time. According to ThinkMobiles, 118 million AR apps were downloaded in 2012, and they predicted that this number would rise to 3.5 billion by 2017.[8] New start-ups pop up everywhere and tech giants spend huge amounts of cash on developing or buying the most promising ventures.

It would be easy to show screenshots, but it is better to take in the experience yourself. You can find some impressive AR examples online, like the one with the Pepsi Max bus shelter in New Oxford Street in London (2014), or the Vespa magazine where the scooter comes alive through the smartphone screen. In marketing, AR offers many new possibilities, most of which remain undiscovered. Hyper-reality's video presents a vision of possibilities, with a city saturated in media.

Mixed reality might pair the ease of online shopping with the thrill of augmented real life experience.

AR in retail is not new. Back in 2010 for example, LEGO delivered an engaging AR experience to kids by introducing AR in-store kiosks. Kids simply needed to hold the LEGO box in front of the kiosk's screen, and the finished LEGO emerged as an overlay on the box.[9]

In 2012, Japanese-based retailer Uniqlo introduced augmented trial rooms, letting the customer choose the piece of clothing they want to try on, overlaying the apparel with different colours.[10]

Figure 6.1   QR code: Pepsi Max Bus shelter

Figure 6.2   QR code: Vespa augmented magazine

Figure 6.3   QR code: Hyper-reality

In 2014, Tesco teamed up with Disney to promote a new line of merchandise from the movie *Frozen*. Kids could pick up a sticker folder and bring the stickers to life on their tablet or smartphone, with each one freeing a different character. Using the Tesco Discover AR app, kids could choose a character to take a selfie with.[11]

Want to visualize how your new sofa will look inside your living room? Back in 2013, IKEA created its first catalogue app featuring AR, making it possible to see the products inside your home before buying them. By scanning the catalogue, a variety of products show up. Choose one and you can see if the product fits your space. You create a picture, save it, add it to your shopping list and take that to the IKEA shop.

Figure 6.4   QR code: Disney Frozen sticker folder

In the AR world, every static product catalogue has the capacity to show life-size products in real-life surroundings, positioned at any angle. This 'augmented commerce' is the next step in ecommerce. Augmented commerce is the buying and selling of goods online using AR to visualize products virtually in the real-world environment before purchasing.[12]

The next step in ecommerce is augmented commerce.

More recently, Dutch online retailer Bol.com launched its own experiment with an AR app,[13] helping customers to visualize furniture in position and assess whether it suits their taste. The app contains about 120 pieces of furniture, including couches, tables, chairs and cabinets, in 2D and in 3D. For the latter, the iPhone must be placed in VR glasses. It seems this application paves the way for more AR experiments in online shopping.

Figure 6.5   QR code: Bol.com

Jewellery chain store Chow Sang Sang from Hong Kong uses virtual reality in its stores to increase sales and operational efficiency. Chow Sang Sang focuses on younger customers, using a 'magic mirror' system. Customers can browse the catalogue, choose a piece of jewellery and then try it on in front of the magic mirror, where they can see themselves virtually 'wearing' the piece.

The customer can take a picture or shoot a video and upload the augmented images to social media. Subsequently, an accompanying QR code helps shop assistants to locate the jewellery in the shop's stock. According to Chow Sang Sang, the magic mirror has had a big impact on customer engagement, with 70 per cent of customers going in front of the magic mirror to play around with it.[14]

Figure 6.6   QR code: Magic mirror at Chow Sang San

The Burberry Beauty Box[15] is a new retail concept from fashion brand Burberry, housed in London's Covent Garden. Customers visiting the Burberry Box Shop looking for nail polish can try out the look of different colours on their own fingernails. Customers just have to select their skin tone and then place different polishes onto a radio frequency identification (RFID)-enabled platform, called the Digital Runway Nail Bar.

The display then shows how the nail shades look in real life on their own fingernails. Customers can also explore connections and mix and match between the different Burberry make-up, accessories and fragrance product lines through digitally enhanced in-house experiences.

AR can bring shop windows and other big screens to life, offering new ways to engage with customers.

Retail sectors using AR:

- 60% – furniture;
- 55% – clothes;
- 39% – foods and beverages;
- 35% – footwear;
- 25% – cosmetics;
- 25% – jewellery;
- 22% – toys.

SOURCE Thinkmobiles.com, 2017[16]

AR can bring shop windows and other big screens to life, offering new ways to engage with customers. Customers wearing a headset can 'walk' through a shop and browse products on the shelves, pick them up and try them on.

One disadvantage of headsets is their bulkiness – although I would have said the same thing about mobile telephones ten years ago! Headsets still remain quite immersive for an integrated store experience.[17] All innovative real-life and online mixes are allowed, since AR expands the customer experience from the physical shop to the augmented mobile screen.

The most important thread, however, is AR being exploited as a gadget. When you want to bring customers to the store, the augmented experience really needs to boost the customer experience linked to the store environment. Online retailers will not sit and wait. Why take your AR mobile app to the store and try on some virtual jeans when you can do the same on the big TV screen at home?

Yihaodian for example, China's largest online grocer, joined forces with Ogilvy & Mather Advertising to set up 1,000 virtual stores in parking lots, parks and in front of iconic landmarks,[18] even on The Great Wall.[19] And they did it overnight.

Not one single store is made of bricks and mortar. Every one of them is 100 per cent virtual and completely invisible for people who aren't connected to the Yihaodian Virtual Store app. The grocery store only appears on your smartphone. You enter the store and browse the aisles for products, then tap the groceries you want, buy them and have them delivered to your home.[20]

Figure 6.7   QR code: Yihaodian's Virtual Stores

While the customer journey is moving online, we should not forget that in many cases the offline part – visiting shops and trade shows, being targeted by billboards and promotional action – is of equal importance in the overall customer journey. Recent developments in shop and retail experience capabilities allow companies to extend customer enchantment to the shop floor. In particular, the possibilities of Large Format Printing, holograms, 3D printing and interactive displays allow for very creative solutions, making shop visits a pure joy.

In this context, a retail consultant recently suggested asking for an entrance fee for shopping malls, following the reasoning that a shopping mall is no longer just a place to shop but has become an experience centre, similar to a Disney-style attraction.

Belgian construction company Willemen Building adopts virtual reality in its 'Step into Your Future' campaign. Glasses immerse you in a virtual world, where you can visit three major projects in a matter of minutes. During your virtual escapade, project leaders explain what you see. One moment you seem to walk the top of the 170-meter-high Astro-tower in Brussels; the next you find yourself under a motorway bridge near Bruges. In 2016, the campaign was awarded a Belgian HR Pioneer Award.

Figure 6.8   QR code: Willemen Group VR

TenCate Outdoor Fabrics produce technical fabrics for safety, sustainability and comfort –waterproof, flame resistant or protecting against challenging climates. With its virtual reality app, they offer customers an immersive experience around their range of products. The app takes you on tour inside the TenCate future factory and you can learn how a digital printer prints the different designs on the fabric. Maintenance tips and contact information are also available through the app.

Figure 6.9   QR code: TenCate Outdoor Fabrics Virtual Reality app

Ici Paris XL is a leading cosmetics retailer in Belgium. The retail brand is part of AS Watsos, a leading global retailing group with more than 12,000 outlets. The challenge for ICI Paris XL, founded in the late 1960s, was to move from a model based on customer care driven by shop assistants towards independent, customer-driven shopping experiences.

In the traditional model, shop assistants would help you through every aspect of your visit, from the moment you crossed the entrance door until check-out and payment. Joost van Bergeyck, the marketing and customer experience director at AS Watson, decided to question this approach and to experiment with a model of customer emancipation.

In the new model, customers are coached in a mixed online and offline world to build a cosmetics profile and discover new products in a playful way. Setting up the new approach required the creation of an integrated CRM and content management tool, plus a redesign of the shops. The model uses active data-driven collaboration with suppliers to develop specific custom-made promotions and to create unique customer experiences.

The implementation is done in a step-by-step way, opening pilot shops and rolling out tests with data-driven, one-to-one communication with customers. Shop assistants become specialist advisors, able to spend much more time with customers in need of assistance, rather than salespeople following shoppers' every move.

At CPI, we believe in the power of interactive point of sales. Our absolute favourite is a holographic display from our partner RetailCommunicators, using prismatic glass product display casing that can be augmented by holographic images. These images are activated with a push of the button or by movement sensing. In the most advanced versions of this technology, the holographic image can be linked to a smartphone, making it possible to control the image.

Notes

1 Sinha-Roy, Piya and Richwine, Lisa [accessed May 2017] Virtual reality sweeps shoppers into new retail dimension, *Reuters* [Online] http://www.reuters.com/article/us-retail-virtualreality-idUSKBN0P210320150623

2 Augment [accessed May 2017] Augmented Reality Dictionary: 5 Terms You Need to Know [Online] http://www.augment.com/blog/augmented-reality-dictionary/

3 Rouse, Margaret [accessed May 2017] What is virtual reality?, *WhatIs.com* [Online] http://whatis.techtarget.com/definition/virtual-reality

4 Wikipedia [accessed May 2017] Augmented reality [Online] https://en.wikipedia.org/wiki/Augmented_reality

5 Wikipedia [accessed May 2017] Augmented reality

6 Reality Technologies [accessed May 2017] How Reality Technology is Used in Shopping [Online] http://www.realitytechnologies.com/shopping

7 Hidden Creative [accessed May 2017] The Future of Augmented Reality, *YouTube* [Online] https://www.youtube.com/watch?v=tnRJaHZH9lo

8 ThinkMobiles [accessed May 2017] Augmented Reality in Retail [Online] https://thinkmobiles.com/augmented-reality-retail/

9 Augment [accessed May 2017] The Top Examples of AR in Retail [Online] http://www.augment.com/blog/best-of-ar-in-retail/

10 Augment [accessed May 2017] The Top Examples of AR in Retail

11 Engine Creative [accessed May 2017] Tesco brings Disney Frozen to life with Augmented Reality magic [Online] http://www.enginecreative.co.uk/blog/tesco-brings-disney-frozen-life-augmented-reality-magic

12 Augment [accessed May 2017] Augmented Commerce [Online] http://www.augment.com/what-is-augmented-commerce/

13 bol.com [accessed May 2017] Bol.com experimenteert met augmented reality (AR) [Online] https://pers.bol.com/2017/02/bol-com-experimenteert-augmented-reality-ar/

14 Intel.com [accessed May 2017] Virtual Reality in Stores Redefines Retail Experiences [Online] http://www.intel.com/content/www/us/en/retail/solutions/videos/magic-mirror-retail-solution-video.html

15 Retail Innovation [accessed May 2017] Burberry's new store introduces the digital nail bar and mobile POS [Online] http://retail-innovation.com/burberrys-new-store-introduces-the-digital-nail-bar-and-mobile-pos

16 ThinkMobiles [accessed May 2017]

17 Magliocca, Evan [accessed May 2017] Retailers need to reassess augmented reality, virtual reality, *Retail Dive* [Online] http://www.retaildive.com/ex/mobilecommercedaily/retailers-need-to-reassess-augmented-reality-virtual-reality

18 Eliot, Lance [accessed May 2017] Retail's new reality: Invisible shopping centers and virtual assistants, *CNBC* [Online] http://www.cnbc.com/2015/04/24/retails-new-reality-four-ways-technology-can-boost-sales-commentary.html

19 Fung, Wendy [accessed May 2017] E-Commerce grocer Yihaodian opens 1,000 stores overnight, *WPP* [Online] http://www.wpp.com/wpp/press/2012/oct/19/ecommerce-grocer-yihaodian-opens-stores-overnight/

20 Fung, Wendy [accessed May 2017]

PART FOUR
Lead, follow or get out of the way

Executing dynamic disruption and perpetual readiness

07

> What will the future bring? The domain in which singularity is already making its presence most keenly felt is sales, marketing and customer service.

21st-century selling

Raymond Kurzweil is a true computer genius and a pioneer in the field of artificial intelligence. He is the main inventor of optical character recognition (OCR), developed the first flatbed scanner and the first text-to-speech synthesizer. The combination of these inventions led to the first text-to-speech reading machine for the blind.

After he sold his first company – Kurzweil Computer Products – to Xerox, Kurzweil set about the development of the first music synthesizer that could imitate all acoustic instruments in a realistic way. He was also the man behind the idea that people would one day speak to computers, with their voice being registered and recognized. He later sold his speech synthesizer technology to Lernaut & Hauspie.[1]

Technological singularity

Kurzweil is now 67 years of age and still works as Director of Engineering at Google. Each day he swallows over 150 vitamin pills and all different kinds of nutritional supplements. He wants to live as long as he can, preferable

Figure 7.1   'Singularity is near': Ray Kurzweil

SOURCE JD Lasica at Poptech, posted on Flickr on October 13, 2006, reproduced under Creative Commons 2.0

until technology makes it possible for human beings to live forever. He is convinced that this will one day be possible.

In 2001, Kurzweil wrote an essay entitled *The Law of Accelerating Returns*.[2] In this essay, he foresaw that Gordon Moore's Law would soon become widespread and generally applicable. Moore was one of the founders of Intel and in 1965 he predicted that the number of transistors on an electric chip would double each year. In 1975, he revised his prediction to every two years.

In reality, the exact number of years is not important. What matters is that computing power is increasing exponentially at a rapid rate. According to Kurzweil, this process has already been taking place for decades and will only get quicker in the future. Just as importantly, ever-quicker computers make possible ground-breaking technology in other fields. In other words, we will not experience 100 years of change during the 21st century, but 20,000 years of change!

Within a decade or so, Kurzweil believes that the intelligence of machines will surpass the intelligence of humans. This is why Kurzweil is regarded as one of the fathers of the concept of 'technological singularity'.[3] The artificial intelligence of computers will soon be many times more powerful than human intelligence. As a result, they will take their further development into their own hands.

Some people think this is fantastic. Others think it is pure fantasy. Be that as it may, Kurzweil has been making predictions about technology for many years – and most of them have come true.[4] For example, in *The Age of Intelligent Machines*,[5] he foresaw that the internet would change the world and would give people wireless access to an international network of libraries, data and information. He predicted that computers would acquire a dominant position in the classroom, intelligently adjusting teaching material to the level of the student. He also argued that one day the individualization of products to meet the specific needs of individual customers would become standard.

In 1999, in *The Age of Spiritual Machines*,[6] he wrote that by 2009 most books would be read from a screen instead of from paper; that driverless cars would become commonplace; that computers would become small enough to fit onto a ring or a credit card; that people would wear or carry portable computers to monitor their health or show them the way to where they want to go; that smart specs would be able to pick up and relay many different kinds of information gathered from the immediate surroundings.[7] And so the list goes on.

Figure 7.2   QR code: Kurzweil's predictions on Wikipedia

According to Kurzweil, the real seminal change will take place after 2040.[8] By then, non-biological intelligence will be several billion times smarter than our limited biological intelligence. In 2045, a $1,000 computer be will more intelligent than all the world's human intelligence combined. When this happens, technological innovation will be taken over by machines, which can think, act and communicate so quickly that a normal person will no longer be able to understand what is happening.

Kurzweil says that we do not need to be afraid of this intelligence, because by then people will also be cybernetically programmed with software installed into their bodies. In other words, people themselves will become more and more like machines. Just like the Borg in *Star Trek*.

HAL's message

In *2001: A Space Odyssey*, Stanley Kubrick's iconic 1968 film of Arthur C Clarke's book, the computer HAL plays a leading role. HAL – one letter short of IBM – stands for *Heuristically programmed ALgorithmic computer*; in other words, artificial intelligence.

The computer with the all-seeing red eye controls all the systems on the spaceship Discovery One on its journey to Jupiter. At a certain moment, HAL discovers a fault in the AE-35 guidance unit. He does not tell astronauts David Bowman and Frank Poole that the unit is already defective, but warns them instead that it will become defective in the near future: '*I've just picked up a fault in the AE35 unit. It's going to go 100 per cent failure in 72 hours.*' Later, HAL discovers that he may have made a mistake and becomes paranoid, which takes the story of the film in a completely different direction.[9]

Whereas HAL's mechanical prescience was pure science fiction back in 1968, nowadays it is a reality. If you wait too long before updating the software on your home computer, you will soon get messages on your screen that these updates are critical. My software updates are now carried out automatically, machine to machine. Once you signal your agreement to the general conditions, the rest is taken out of your hands. We live in a world where we need to get used to complying with the instructions of our machines.

> We live in a world where we need to get used to complying with the instructions of our machines.

The internet of things

2045 is still some years away. Even so, we have all already experienced the rapid progress being made by automation and computerization in our daily lives. And we quickly forget what life was like before the internet, smartphones, Google and Facebook. Soon drones will be delivering packages to your house. Smart algorithms will also be taking over many other tasks performed by people. Ordering a book or reserving a hotel online now involves no human interaction whatsoever. Your order or reservation (and your personal profile) is processed automatically in a customer management system by Amazon.com, Bol.com or Booking.com.

And it doesn't stop there. Smart cars, smart wearables, smart spectacles, smart televisions, smart toasters, smart clothing, smart fridges, smart toothbrushes, smart cameras, smart electricity meters, smart thermostats, smart containers, smart check-in desks, smart labelling, smart paint, and smart machines of a thousand and one different kinds, each exchanging information online and all contactable via the latest equally smart app. They exist. Already. The internet is no longer the privileged domain of us humans.

Today, the world contains some 4.9 billion smart devices that collect and communicate user data – according to figures from the Gartner Research Institute.[10] It is estimated that by 2020 no fewer than 13 billion things equipped with telematics and geolocation technology will be trawling cyberspace for user data. They will share this huge mass of information with each other and with countless different data systems around the world. Add to this the activities of business and government, and you actually end up somewhere nearer a total of 25 billion.[11]

The internet is increasingly becoming the playground of everyone and everything. Before very much longer, every piece of equipment in your house or office will be connected to the web. It is even possible that your unhappy kitchen robot, lying criminally underused in your kitchen cupboard, will one day place an advert for its own sale on eBay! And that it will be collected by drone once it has found a new – and more gastronomically active – master.

> It is even possible that your criminally underused kitchen robot will one day
> place an advert for its own sale on eBay!

The internet of things can be divided into three separate components, each linked to the other online: the smart devices that record and transmit data; the supplier's data warehouse, where the data is processed; and the analytical software robots, which evaluate the data and automatically generate responses that are re-transmitted to the smart devices and/or their users. In this way, a continuous flow of feedback loops is created between the user of the device, the device itself and the supplier of the device.

96 per cent of the world's 800 most important business leaders intend in the near future to implement new solutions based on the internet of things. 68 per cent claim to have such solutions already in operation. And this while 99 per cent of all the devices in the world today are still not connected.[12]

In the past, a customer bought a device, and that was all the supplier knew. Did the customer ever take it out of the box? And if they did, were they happy with it? These and hundreds of other things remained unknown to the supplier. In the near future, suppliers will be able to tell whether the device is currently on or off, how many hours have passed since it was last used, how frequently it is used, whether it is subject to peaks of use, whether it is in imminent danger of breaking down, and so on. The device itself will automatically tell you all these things (you don't need to ask!) and it will even let you know when it needs to be maintained.

The same is true of stock levels. Intelligent searchers will warn you when stocks are running low and need to be replenished. This signal will be checked against production planning and automatically converted into an order of the correct size, which in turn will be automatically processed and made ready for delivery. Once again without the need for human intervention, even to push a button!

The continuous stream of information about the use and status of your product offers numerous possibilities for further optimizing the customer experience. If you have the necessary tools to analyse all this data effectively, you can monitor non-stop what the customer is doing and what your product is doing (when, where and how), which allows you to take the right responsive action in real time.

There is also huge commercial potential. You can see, for example, if the data of one user differs significantly from other users, which gives you the opportunity to investigate the reason. Once you have found it, you can contact the deviant user with useful proposals. You can also exchange data with other suppliers, so that everyone's general level of service improves, to the benefit of the customers and the sector as a whole.

Similarly, the data of one machine can be combined with the data of another; for example, data from a cooled production unit with data from an airco system, with the aim of improving their shared cooling technology.

Taking matters a stage further, by combining your device data with information obtained from other sources such as social media, you will find it easier to more accurately predict and respond to the needs of your customers. Imagine that a customer lets it be known that they have just won a major new order. Further imagine that your machine – which the customer needs to process that order – tells you that it is currently working to its maximum capacity. You can then pass on this information to the customer, accompanied by interesting commercial propositions that could work to the benefit of both of you.

Automation to automation

The internet of things will have a huge influence on the way the selling process is organized in future. A customer is satisfied with your product or service if it provides the value that was promised. Increasingly, however, the customer will only be satisfied if value is provided throughout the entire length of the customer journey – and not just at the end.

In the past, the tools were not available to measure customer satisfaction constantly. Sporadic personal meetings, telephone calls and occasional market research surveys were insufficient to formulate effective answers to the customer's silent needs. It was like flying blind. Even if the available information was processed in a CRM, that information was never complete and often out-of-date.

As a result, many marketing and commercial actions in the past were based more on gut feeling than anything else. There was a sense that 'something needs to be done', but nobody really knew what. This hit-and-miss approach trusted largely to luck. Sometimes a campaign was successful, reaching the right people at the right time; but more often than not the results were disappointing.

In this book we have repeatedly emphasized that the customer has now taken the lead in the selling process. This applies equally to the customer journey, which has followed a whole new trajectory since the arrival of the 'internet of humans'. If companies wish to optimize the customer experience in this new and complex environment, they can no longer rely on their gut feeling. You need to know precisely what you are doing, when you are doing it, for whom you are doing it, how you are doing it and even whether you might be better doing it later on.

Marketing automation technology makes it possible for you to track the online behaviour of your customers. As a result, you can respond quickly and effectively with made-to-measure proposals that reflect each customer's online activity: their click behaviour, reading behaviour, the way they react to emails and online campaigns, the questions they ask online, the frequency of their visits to web pages, etc.

Marketing automation further makes it possible to automatically convert this data into customer profiles and to update them in real time. This allows you to meet the specific wishes of each customer throughout their sales journey, no matter how long.

> Products themselves will generate huge amounts of data that will further help to optimize the customer experience.

The internet of things adds a whole new dimension to the situation. In the world of smart devices, it is no longer just people who leave traces of their activities. The products themselves also generate huge volumes of non-stop data. This data can be used to help further optimize the customer experience. It is all a question of knowing what you want to do to give added satisfaction.

But that is not an easy question to answer. The data being generated by these devices will turn big data into really big data. You will need to know which signals to respond to and which ones to ignore. Moreover, you can never detach the data transmitted by a device from the customer relationship to which it belongs. When interpreting the data, you will therefore need to take account of both the purchase history and the past behaviour of the customer concerned. It is only when you combine the data from the internet of things with the customer's known online behaviour and profile that the device data will yield commercial added value.

The combination of internet of things technology, marketing automation and CRM offers you a golden opportunity to improve the customer experience. It makes it possible for you to monitor both online customer behaviour and online product behaviour. The resulting data can then be integrated to give you an even better understanding of the customer – an understanding that leads to more value for them and more sales for you. It gives you the option of organizing feedback loops not only to the customer, but also to the smart device. In this way, the device also becomes the medium for your marketing message.

Sales, marketing and customer service are therefore no longer about simply making people happy; they are about making machines happy as well. A smart device that informs you continuously of its status gives you the opportunity to keep that machine happy (ie in perfect running order), which also makes the customer happy. What's more, it is an opportunity you had better take. Customers know that machines now report everything back to their makers, and so they not unreasonably expect these makers to act in good time to deal with any problems before they arise.

This means, for example, that customers will soon expect suppliers to tell them when their machines need maintaining or their stocks replenishing. What's more, they will expect this, without delay, without inconvenience and almost without any customer input whatsoever. The supplier's own operational organization will need to take full and timely account of these expectations.

We can therefore expand our definition in the previous paragraph: sales, marketing and customer service are no longer about attracting new customers, but about keeping them and the products they use happy over the entire length of the customer journey and the product life cycle.

This further means that whereas in the past the optimizing of the customer relationship was largely a matter of human-to-human interaction, in future it will increasingly become a combination of automation-to-human and, with the continuing expansion of the internet of things, automation-to-automation. Human-to-human will disappear from the equation almost completely

The next obvious evolution is the use of artificial intelligence. With Amelia, IPsoft have created a robot that can conduct parallel conversations with multiple customers in different languages. Based on the contexts in which certain words are used and the questions that are asked, Amelia can also decide whether or not the caller is feeling stressed. If stress is detected, the call is forwarded to a human operator. Once the call is completed, Amelia makes a report about the content of the conversation and the solution proposed, so that the next contact with the customer is based on full knowledge of the situation. Amelia understands what customers want and what they feel in relation to that want.

The widespread use of Amelia and her cybernetic friends is not as far off as you might think. At the time of writing, different Dutch and Belgian companies are in contact with IPsoft to explore the possibilities of this application. At this stage, the general feeling is that Amelia's strengths can best be exploited when working in tandem with a human operative.

Imagine you had a colleague who has memorized all the service manuals, who knows the answer to every frequently asked question, who can simultaneously conduct up to four thousand parallel conversations in different languages, but is still prepared to occasionally make use of your human skills, because she is 'only' a robot? Wouldn't you want such a colleague? Wouldn't it make your job that much easier?

Figure 7.3 Amelia marks the transition from robots in the factory to robots in the office

SOURCE ©IPsoft

Collaboration between people and robots is an area of increasing interest, as evidenced by the devotion of the entire June 2015 edition of the *Harvard Business Review* to this issue. Under the title *Meet your new employee – How to manage the man-machine collaboration*,[13] the review examined the likely benefits and problems associated with robotics in a commercial environment. How would you feel if you were given instructions by a robot? Would it help if that robot had a realistic human appearance? Yes, according to a recent survey. Is there a risk of becoming emotionally attached to robots? Yes again, or so it seems.

As a result, a group of HR specialists are already engaged in writing a set of rules of conduct for interacting correctly with intelligent robots in an office setting. There is even a special task force to decide how to deal with inappropriate behaviour on the part of human staff towards their humanoid colleagues.

Research shows that the risk of machines becoming the victim of harassment is not as far-fetched as it might sound. Precisely what this might involve, I will leave to the reader's imagination. But Apple's Siri will know exactly what I mean. Numerous blogs have already been devoted to the question of whether or not this digital assistant has been programmed to deal with sexually tinted questions. Such is the stuff of urban legend!

Legend or not, the possibility that you will one day soon be using a robot to answer your mails and develop your marketing campaigns is no longer pie in the sky. And once your action is assessed for its value by the customer's own robot operative, which will then decide whether to accept your proposal or not, we are getting very close to full singularity in marketing.

Don't worry; we will keep you posted. Just watch our blog!

Robots working in sales, marketing and customer service will soon be a common sight. Robots telling people where their priorities lie will be with us before you know it. It is not as unlikely as you probably think!

My bot talks to your bot, and they get along fine

The growing shift in communication preference from speech to text has led to the growth of chatbots. This has a major impact on the way customer conversations will be handled in the future. People who master multitasking and texting are able to handle simultaneous demands through email, messages and engage in three or four conversations at the same time.

This leads to an increased productivity in both call and contact centres, allowing people to use an augmented version of themselves.

The next step is to leave the human interaction out of the equation completely, replacing your customer care agent with a bot who can answer most of the questions better and faster. Especially when an increasing level of contextual understanding and semantic knowledge has been added to the robotic competences, as is the case with a number of customer care bots that are currently on the market.

Chatbots and other intelligent assistants are gaining grip, particularly because the mobile customer likes this form of interaction, making them well suited for this mobile use.[14]

That said, people still want a 'human touch';[15] an escape route giving access to a human assistant. Yet the intelligent bot is also offering this level of authenticity by remembering prior conversations, using your name in the conversation or by adding other elements to disguise the robotic character of the conversation.

'The Chatbot Explainer' is a more international survey,[16] performed by UK-based Business Insider, which revealed that 38 per cent of consumers rated their overall perception of chatbots as positive and only 11 per cent reported a negative experience. The survey spoke to more than 5,000 consumers from Australia, France, Germany, Japan, the US and the UK.

Perceptions varied heavily by country. French consumers seemed the most receptive, with 50 per cent of consumers having a positive attitude towards talking to bots. European countries in general seem more receptive compared to the US and Japan. Although the majority of consumers still prefer human assistance today, this will shift rapidly when younger 'text natives' enter the labour and consumer age.

All the same, more than half of consumers globally (56 per cent) reported still preferring to speak with a human instead of getting assistance from a chatbot. The survey therefore concludes that businesses should focus on utility rather than adding a personality to the chatbot.[17]

In the Aspect survey, 58 per cent say bots are best for simple to moderate questions. The large bulk (86 per cent) of respondents insist on having the option to transfer to an agent.[18] Another survey by HubSpot confirms a decrease in openness to bots when the customer's problem complexity rises.[19] The most effective usage for chatbots is when customer queries are simple and need very few steps, like wanting to change their billing address or when they require the company's contact details.

With more technical multistep questions, people prefer human assistance. In those cases, another survey indicates that receptiveness drops to 26 per cent.[20] The HubSpot survey also revealed a bot sitting on a company's website, giving the visitor a direct answer to questions like 'What's your pricing?', or 'What's your company phone number?' would be very much appreciated. More than half of respondents (57 per cent) were interested in getting real-time answers from bots on a company website.[21]

When a Dutch bank built a chatbot into its customer portal, it proved to be an instant success. In no time, 84 per cent of customers used the chat box to raise their question. Add to this the capability to analyse these questions and map the information people are looking for, and you can easily detect question patterns and identify FAQs. One step further and you introduce a chatbot. Two more, the bot analyses the questions and adds parts of the question in its answer, making the customer experience more useful and enjoyable.

Yet another three or more steps and you end up with an even smarter voice bot like Amelia from IPSoft; as a cognitively aware agent she builds segments of personal information into her answer using natural language, making it virtually impossible to discern her answer from that of a human help desk worker.

The rise of the automated chatbots will redefine the customer service industry altogether, replacing some traditional human-to-human operations.[22] With an AI-powered bot, businesses have a 24/7 salesperson on hand that can interact with customers on a one-to-many basis.[23] Chatbots will therefore reduce conversation time and boost efficiency gains.

On the receiving end, chatbots will also eliminate waiting times for the customer. A recent study by Juniper Research[24] indicates healthcare and banking sector could benefit the most. It says to expect dramatic cost savings in the range of 50 to 70 cents (USD) per interaction.

On average, a chatbot enquiry could save over four minutes compared to traditional call centres. App-based bot interactions are likely to be most successful, while SMS chatbots are more useful for mass messaging.[25] The study says many chatbots are suited for enquiries such as healthcare diagnosis, where users can select predefined answers, allowing bots to assess health issues and provide a recommended course of action.

As AI capabilities advance, bots will also be able to assist in more sophisticated healthcare diagnostics, such as monitoring and analysis of mental health. Juniper also predicts that the success rate of bot interactions in the healthcare sector will move from 12 per cent currently to over 75 per cent in 2022. In the banking sector, Juniper expects this success rate to reach over 90 per cent in 2022.[26]

Asking and prepping your sales bot to strike the best deal possible for your next business move, competing with other bots, might well become the business game of tomorrow. Today, bot communication through chat-based platforms is aimed at bot-to-consumer interaction. This means the bot's communication is focused on you. But at some point in time, not so far from now, we will enter the age of bot-to-bot communication and at that moment, bots will also start to negotiate with and learn from each other.

> At some point in time, not so distant future, we will enter the age of bot-to-bot communication.

Once you start thinking in a bot-to-bot communication frame, a whole range of new possibilities opens up, causing a major paradigm shift in customer service and ecommerce. Imagine a bot that needs to answer a rather complex question from a customer. The bot searches its smart database, but lacks a piece of essential information.

At that point, the bot could engage other bots in its network to be of assistance and dig in their own backend systems, combining all intelligence available and getting the job done.

> Once you start thinking in a bot-to-bot communication frame, a whole range of new possibilities opens up.

One step further, and instead of you looking for the right product at the right price, your personal bot, armed with some artificial intelligence, might conclude that, based on your real-time profile dataset, data from your internet-of-things fridge and some further analytics, you are in need of a certain product at a certain price.

Your bot then might just take the initiative to start an online search, communicating and negotiating with other bots, in order to find and deliver the goods at the best price possible. Your bot will even insert your personal preferences into the negotiations and for example, negotiate a delivery at 10.15 am. This would not be because you shared your agenda, but because the bot will have taken your stress level and previous related behaviour into account, predicting a 55 per cent chance you will want to spend some early morning time running in the woods.

The beauty of bot-robot-communication is that it will not be in code but in easily understandable language.[27] Therefore it will also be easy to join any bot-to-bot conversation.

Looking for an appropriate bot to serve your needs? Just search online. First, search engines are geared towards surfacing chat app platforms, and they do so by the hundreds. Bing.com displays the bot search results in a dedicated area at the top of the results. Bing users will also be able to search for bots overall and by categories.[28]

Meanwhile on Kik, the bot shop, you can shop for a chatbot. The choices of bots are listed in categories ranging from 'Fun with friends' and 'Entertainment' to 'Meet new people' and 'Fashion and Beauty'. You can chat with a nonstop Chuck Norris bot, have a conversation with anonymous people on Sensay, chat on H&M for instant outfit inspiration, practice self-care on Shine, chat to Sephora to learn about makeup, and so on.

Figure 7.4   QR code: Kik, the bot shop

Crystalknows

Today, marketing and communication is all about mass personalization. But how do you engage with people you don't (or barely) know – considering that personalization is not only about content or the offer itself, but more about connection and tone of voice?

US-based Crystal Project Inc. was founded in 2014 by Drew D'Agostino, who previously co-founded Attend.com, innovating event management software solutions. Attend.com helps event organizers produce high-quality events by simplifying and automating event management processes.[29]

Drew D'Agostino developed Crystal with the sole purpose of fixing the communication problems that arise when two people fail to understand their personality differences, especially over email. Its first product, Crystalknows, is an AI tool in Gmail that helps with writing email content in the tone of voice the recipient likes to be addressed. It does so by feeding you real-time suggestions as you compose emails, such as 'use expressive language', 'use lengthy formal language' or 'write clearly and directly'.[30] It tells you how to greet, how you should compose the body of your email and how to sign off.

In normal conversation we adjust our tone of voice and the way we speak by capturing all kinds of signals, for example tone of voice, rhythm, phrasing and body language. We sense nervousness, boredom, excitement, alertness, contentment... But online conversations cut us off from this emotional apparatus. Crystal aims to fill in that gap by looking at an individual's personality characteristics using online information about their online behaviour.

Based on its existing database and the extra info you provide about yourself and the other person, several algorithms help to build a personality score for both you and the person you would like to contact. The model is based on matching your score with one of the 54 personality types in the Crystalknows database. After choosing a personality type, Crystal shows you a personality summary, along with advice on how to address that person.[31] Tools are based on DISC assessment, using four primary personality types to determine behaviour: dominant, influential, steady and calculating.[32]

This might all sound a bit disturbing, but Crystal only analyses the writing style of the public information that shows up on blogs and sites like LinkedIn, Twitter, Yelp, and reviews on Amazon.com. It only uses our public language patterns, the information behind the information we publish ourselves. The new reality however is one where deciphering our personality is not the work of experts anymore, but that of a bot, and its work is out there in the open. Could be interesting for sales, don't you think?

Crystal offers a free, unlimited practice account, but you can upgrade to get premium features like real-time email suggestions and corrections, relationship predictions, example email templates and team/organizational analysis. Crystal is also thinking about proactive functionalities, such as sending you tips prior to your meeting to help you prepare your tone of voice.[33]

Figure 7.5 Crystalknows

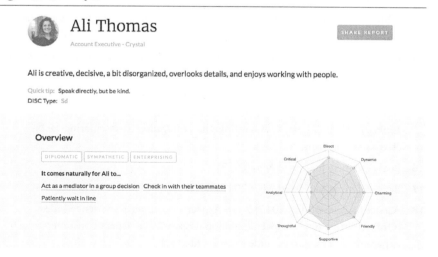

SOURCE With thanks to Crystal

Notes

1 Wikipedia [accessed September 2015] Raymond Kurzweil [Online] https://nl.wikipedia.org/wiki/Raymond_Kurzweil

2 Kurzweil, R [accessed June 2015] The Law of Accelerating Returns, *Kurzweil Accelerating Intelligence* [Online] http://www.kurzweilai. net/the-law-of-accelerating-returns

3 Wikipedia [accessed June 2015] Technologische singulariteit [Online] https://nl.wikipedia.org/wiki/Technologische_singulariteit

4 Wikipedia [accessed August 2015] Predictions made by Ray Kurzweil [Online] https://en.wikipedia.org/wiki/Predictions_made_by_Ray_Kurzweil

5 Kurzweil, Raymond (1990) *The Age of Intelligent Machines*, MIT Press, Boston

6 Kurzweil, Raymond (1992) *The Age of Spiritual Machines*, Viking, New York

7 Wikipedia [accessed August 2015] Predictions made by Ray Kurzweil

8 Wikipedia [accessed August 2015] Predictions made by Ray Kurzweil

9 Wikipedia [accessed September 2015] HAL 9000 [Online] https://en.wikipedia.org/wiki/HAL_9000

10 Gartner [accessed June 2015] Gartner Says 4.9 Billion Connected 'Things' Will Be in Use in 2015 [Online] http://www.gartner.com/newsroom/id/2905717

11 Gartner [accessed June 2015]

12 SALESManago [accessed Dec 2017] Marketing Automation – The Definitive and Ultimate Guide to Marketing Automation [Online] https://www.salesmanago.com/info/definitve_and_ultimate_new_knowledge.htm

13 HBR (2015) Meet your new employee: How to manage the man-machine collaboration, *Harvard Business Review*, June

14 Beaver, Laurie [accessed May 2017] Chatbots are gaining traction, *Business Insider* [Online] http://uk.businessinsider.com/chatbots-are-gaining-traction-2017-5

15 Kim, Larry [accessed May 2017] 10 Fascinating Facts About Chatbots, *LinkedIn* [Online] https://www.linkedin.com/pulse/10-fascinating-facts-chatbots-larry-kim

16 Beaver, Laurie [accessed May 2017]

17 Beaver, Laurie [accessed May 2017]

18 Aspect [accessed May 2017] 2016 Aspect Consumer Experience Index [Online] https://www.aspect.com/globalassets/2016-aspect-consumer-experience-index-survey_index-results-final.pdf

19 An, Mimi [accessed May 2017] Artificial Intelligence Is Here – People Just Don't Realize It, *HubSpot* [Online] https://research.hubspot.com/reports/artificial-intelligence-is-here

20 An, Mimi [accessed May 2017]

21 An, Mimi [accessed May 2017]

22 Violino, Bob [accessed May 2017] Chatbots driving down costs in customer service, *Digital Insurance* [Online] https://www.dig-in.com/news/chatbots-driving-down-costs-in-customer-service

23 An, Mimi [accessed May 2017]

24 Juniper Research [accessed May 2017] Chatbots, a game changer for banking & healthcare, saving $8 billion annually by 2022 [Online] https://www.juniperresearch.com/press/press-releases/chatbots-a-game-changer-for-banking-healthcare

25 Juniper Research [accessed May 2017]

26 Nelissen, Niko [accessed May 2017] How bot-to-bot could soon replace APIs, *VentureBeat* [Online] https://venturebeat.com/2016/06/05/how-bot-to-bot-could-soon-replace-apis/

27 Johnson, Khari [accessed May 2017] Bing now serves up bots from Facebook Messenger, Slack, and other chat apps, *VentureBeat* [Online] https://venturebeat.com/2017/05/12/bing-now-serves-up-bots-from-facebook-messenger-slack-and-other-chat-apps/

28 Johnson, Khari [accessed May 2017] Microsoft's Bing search results now include Skype bots, *VentureBeat* [Online] https://venturebeat.com/2017/05/10/microsofts-bing-search-results-now-include-bots/

29 Attend.com [accessed May 2017] Attend.com Integrates Event Management Solution into Leading CRM Applications [Online] https://www.attend.com/home/pr_salesforce_blackbaud_integration.html

30 Crystal [accessed May 2017] Meet your communication coach [Online] https://www.crystalknows.com

31 Metz, Rachel [accessed May 2017] Can You Improve Your E-Mails by Analyzing Recipients' Personalities?, *MIT Technology Review* [Online] https://www.technologyreview.com/s/537256/can-you-improve-your-e-mails-by-analyzing-recipients-personalities/

32 Crystal [accessed May 2017]

33 Ramli, June [accessed May 2017] Crystalknows, a software that helps a person write emails the correct way, *Elite Agent* [Online] https://eliteagent.com.au/crystalknows-software-helps-person-write-emails-correct-way/

The new age of disruptive selling – from reading to doing

08

> If you want to introduce disruptive selling and reorganize your entire commercial organization, starting from a blank sheet of paper, you will need to have a plan of action.

Output

Sales is changing. And that change is driven by four factors, factors that mutually influence and reinforce each other.

Factor 1: marketing technology

Marketing automation makes it possible to obtain deeper insights into the needs, expectations and wishes of prospects and customers. The use of this technology enables companies to deal with customers on a personalized, made-to-measure basis for the very first time, and during each phase of the customer journey. The impact of marketing technology will be further strengthened by the internet of things.

Factor 2: the consumer

Today's commercial customers buy differently. They want to find in B2B what they can now find in B2C. The customer has taken the lead in the selling process and expects to experience personalized value 24 hours a day, seven days a week. This requires a new commercial organization, in which sales, marketing and customer service work together in an integrated process, in close collaboration with product management and value delivery. The values that will make this new organization successful are the Three As: agility, accountability and authenticity.

Factor 3: the employee

The modern employee or the modern team member wants to develop his or her potential through a process of lifelong learning. A growing number of professionals want to decide who they will work for, when and where. People nowadays look differently at work and wish to avoid boring, repetitive jobs. They expect meaning and satisfaction.

This necessitates a different approach to the concept of responsibility. The organization must become much more transparent. Everyone must be both agile and accountable. Managers must facilitate, instead of attempting to command and control. Technology makes it possible to link results to the performance of individual members of staff.

Technology will also make a large number of jobs redundant, but at the same time will create new ones, linked to implementation and administration of a new technology-driven business model in a technology-driven society.

Factor 4: the organization

Companies not only need to deal with new technology and new consumers, but also with the new expectations of their own people. This will require retraining, both in technical matters and in terms of general attitudes and skills. The company and its personnel will need to commit to lifelong learning.

Choosing the technology

If you intend to redesign your commercial organization from scratch, you need to set the bar high. Take as your starting point the basic idea that you want to manage your customer relationships without any human interaction from the company side. Which tasks can you automate? Which tasks then remain for sales, marketing and customer service? Which functionalities will these three departments need to carry out these tasks? Which tools and metrics are necessary to make your organization more authentic, accountable and agile?

Take as your starting point the basic idea that you want to manage your customer relationships without any human interaction from the company side.

Selecting the technology is relatively simple. All you need to know is precisely what you want to achieve and then carefully screen (or have screened) the various options in the marketplace. There are plenty of experts who can help you in this. In Chapter 5 I gave you a number of guidelines to help you make your choices in a focused manner.

But remember that the market is evolving all the time. For this reason, it is wise not be too hasty in making your decision. Make a wishlist by all means, but review it at your leisure, so that it can ripen over a period of time. Involve your staff. Carry out tests and evaluations. Discover what data and tools you still need. If you are a technology manager, keep your finger on the pulse and follow the latest market developments – even once your initial choice has been made. Your system will need to evolve continually, if you want to carry on giving valuable experiences to your customers far into the future.

The worth of some practices and tools will be confirmed. Others will need to be scrapped or upgraded. In a disruptive selling environment, you regularly need to review all your decisions – about everything!

Once you have made your choice, introducing a new tool can be done quite quickly. Results are assessed, the method of working evaluated, different models tested, choices confirmed or amended, a subscription arranged, software downloaded – and away you go! In the chapter on 'People and resources', I described how an implementation cycle of 18 weeks for a new tool is both reasonable and achievable. Longer is not a good idea, because people start to find it boring. And boring never works – not for your customers and not for your own staff.

Setting up a new commercial structure is a different matter. Changes involving people and procedures that influence each other are less simple – and more sensitive.

People

In Chapter 4, I also looked in detail at the changes in functions and responsibilities that the new organizational structure will make necessary. Old methods of working will need to be unlearnt. New approaches will need to be absorbed and assimilated, including new technology and new ways of steering the sales process. This means understanding new concepts, learning to work with them and their associated tools, and, ultimately, achieving the results that justify the changes.

It also means, as previously mentioned, being willing to continually re-evaluate existing strategy, existing task distribution, existing methods and existing technology. Old certainties must be replaced by new ideas.

The integration of the different processes of marketing, sales and customer service demands a high level of flexibility from the personnel involved. Not everyone reacts well to this kind of environment. For many organizations, the necessary changes also involve a complete change of culture, with the old way of doing things being replaced by a radically new – and for some, alien – way of doing things. Members of staff who initially seem to be ambassadors of change can sometimes begin to doubt and even despair, once the change becomes more concrete and rumour and gossip begin to circulate.

The valley of despair

People go through various stages of emotion when they are subjected to change. Even the people who applaud loudest when change is first announced can soon become doubters, once it becomes clearer what that change actually means and once the rumours and the gossip begin to fly. Change confronts your staff with the unexpected and the unknown – and there are very few people who are comfortable with these phenomena.

As a result, the majority of your personnel will probably experience a feeling of despair at some point in the process.[1] This begins with a growing uncertainty: 'Can I really cope with this?' Uncertainty gradually becomes fear: 'What impact will this have on me?' Suddenly, the change has become a threat, something that needs to be denied. These reactions are natural.

As a manager, it is your task to ensure that your employees do not fall too deep into despair, so that they actually begin to sabotage the change or end up with depression. You can best do this by emphasizing the positive aspects of the change, by helping them to see the benefits it can bring for them (shorter hours, greater responsibility, more job satisfaction, etc).

In this respect, change is just another product that needs to be sold – with your employees as the customers. And as with any other customers, you need to take them on a journey. You must provide them with an individually tailored experience every step of the way. In this way, value and trust can gradually grow as you move forward together through your sales funnel.

In this book I have also underlined the value of working with objectives and key results. This is an approach which, if correctly applied, offers the huge benefit of being able to translate the ambitions of the organization into easily recognizable individual goals and targets. By agreeing concrete personal targets that contribute to the bigger picture, each member of staff becomes conscious of the role that he or she plays in the company's success. Clarity in respect of these targets will also lead to a further growth in confidence and trust, showing as it does the company's faith in the employee to achieve the required level of performance.

Trust is also essential if you want to build a new and fully integrated organization. Working with clear individual objectives and key results, combined with giving staff the necessary responsibility and freedom of manoeuvre in return for accepting personal accountability based on those results, is crucial for the buy-in of your staff to the change process.

The implementation plan

To work through such a process, in which your organization needs to reinvent itself and develop a whole new technological approach, it is necessary to have a project plan; in this case, an implementation plan. This includes all the necessary step-by-step actions and positions them on a time line. The implementation deals with processes, organization and technology, but also with positioning, communication management and communication planning.

When you start the roll-out of a change process, it is important to start with the changes that can give you a number of quick wins. These are changes that are quick and easy to implement, producing immediate results that everyone can see. Quick wins create a positive effect that reduces the level of worry in the organization and builds up confidence in the beneficial effect of change in the longer term.

A number of change elements will probably already have been trialled in a pilot environment. If this is not the case, you need to include a number of new pilot studies for selected key issues in your implementation plan. A pilot project is a useful intermediary step between the decision to change and its actual roll-out. These projects are always set up in a context that is as realistic as possible. This means that the feedback from your people will also be realistic. It gives them the opportunity to acclimatize to the new technologies and processes within the company's new positioning. At the same time, it provides a correct basis for measuring results and taking decisions that will further optimize the change programme.

Part of the implementation of the new way of working and the new technology will need to be spread over a longer period of time. This is necessary to allow the organization to gradually digest the many different changes that will be involved. Additional time will also be required to fine-tune the integration of some of the changes that may not immediately work as planned.

You cannot rebuild your entire organization in a matter of weeks. That may work on paper, but not in practice, where the unpredictable human factor always plays a role. Some of your staff will need extra training or extra motivation. Or you may need to recruit and train new talent from outside the company. And although you will try to avoid it for as long as you can, you may eventually decide that some people need to be let go.

In general, the complete transformation of a medium-sized organization takes between eighteen months and two years. But you need to start seeing the first results after the initial three to four months.

Communication

It is vital that the new method of working is well documented in a manner that encourages the agility you require. For this reason, it is better to work with flow diagrams, stand-up demos and video clips, rather than thick manuals. This allows you to make amendments more easily as the change process progresses, and also allows easy communication of the necessary information.

It is equally important to set up a number of different channels that will allow the key principles of the new sales approach to slowly filter through all layers of the organization. However, it must also be possible for information to move the other way. Managers at all levels must always be prepared to listen to the input, worries, suggestions and uncertainties of their staff. It will often be necessary to adjust aspects of the change process based on the valuable feedback of your own people.

This is a two-way process. The organization must be willing to absorb the step-by-step changes of the implementation plan. But the implementation plan must also be able to absorb the feedback of the organization in relation to those steps. It is for this reason that the implementation plan needs to set out a clear course and timing, but without either of these aspects being set in stone.

Of the numerous elements involved in the change process, good internal communication is perhaps the most vital of all. People need to be able to air their views and concerns. And to do this meaningfully, they also need to be properly informed. Successful change is impossible without transparency. For this reason, it is essential to set up a good internal communication structure, based on tools like Yammer or Slack.

It is also useful to make a series of short videos (with a maximum duration of 60 seconds) in which you explain why certain changes are necessary and how they are going to be carried out. For staff who want a quick overview of the relevant material, infographics are a possible answer, while for those who want to read the full story internal blogs are probably the best option.

The development of personal training trajectories will be necessary for almost everyone. The object of all these measures is to present a clear picture of the change process in images, text and figures. This is the only way to ensure that each employee is able to understand and digest the change narrative in the manner that is most appropriate for him or her.

To avoid confusion during implementation of the change project, it is crucial to continue repeating the core principle over and over again. You can regard this core principle as the mission statement of the project. This one central principle – the objective for which everyone is striving, the reason for its importance and the effect it will create – needs to be formulated very carefully.

Throughout the implementation phase it will be the reference point for every decision taken. This means that you need to get it right. But once you have got it right, you need to keep on hammering home the same message.

This is also why we at CPI always demand leadership of the project whenever a company transformation is involved. When new parties join the project – for example, an advertising bureau that is engaged to set out the creative lines of the new marketing approach, or an implementation company that is hired to programme the CRM – we ensure that this party is locked into the big picture. In this way, we can be certain that everyone is working in the same direction. And if someone tries to move the goalposts with new ideas that are not really necessary or deviate from the agreed line, we make sure that the change programme stays on course and continues to focus on the result it is intended to achieve.

Note

1 Fisher, J M (2015) A Time for Change, *Human Resource Development International*, **8:2**, pp 257–64

INDEX